'In the diocese of Chelmsford, we have always treasured our association with Evelyn Underhill and her love for what is now our House of Retreat at Pleshey. It was therefore tremendously exciting to discover her handwritten collection of prayers. This book now makes those prayers available to everyone. To read them and to pray them through is to enter into the heart and experience the spirituality of one of the most significant Christian writers of the twentieth century.'

Stephen Cottrell, Bishop of Chelmsford

Prière Simple

& all thy people

L ord! make us instruments of thy healing Peace
Where there is hate, that we may bring Love
Where there is offence that we may bring Pardon
Where there is discord that we may bring Union
Where there is error, that we may bring Truth
Where there is doubt, that we may bring Faith.
Where there is despair that we may bring Hope
Where there is darkness that we may bring Light
Where there is sadness, that we may bring Joy

O Master! make us not such so much
To be consoled as Console
To be understood, as to Understand
To be loved, as to love.

For it is in giving that we receives
It is in self-forgetfulness that we finds
It is in pardoning that we are pardoned
It is in dying that we awakes to Eternal Life

attributed to St Francis.   Old French.

A page from Evelyn Underhill's original Prayer Book

EVELYN UNDERHILL'S
PRAYER BOOK

Edited by Robyn Wrigley-Carr

To all retreatants
at the House of Retreat, Pleshey,
past, present and future

First published in Great Britain in 2018

Society for Promoting Christian Knowledge
36 Causton Street
London SW1P 4ST
www.spck.org.uk

British Library Cataloguing-in-Publication Data
A catalogue record for this book is available from the British Library

ISBN 978–0–281–07873–8
eBook ISBN 978–0–281–07874–5

Typeset by Manila Typesetting Company
First printed in Great Britain by Jellyfish Print Solutions
Subsequently digitally reprinted in Great Britain

eBook by Manila Typesetting Company

Produced on paper from sustainable forests

Contents

About the author

Dr Robyn Wrigley-Carr is Senior Lecturer in Theology and Spirituality at Alphacrucis College, Sydney, Australia. She studied for her PhD on the spiritual direction of Baron Friedrich von Hügel at the University of St Andrews, Scotland.

Foreword

What is the basis of our faith?

The Christian life consists in what God does for us, not what we do for God . . . the Christian life consists in what God says to us, not what we say about God. We also, of course, do things and say things, but if we do not return to Square One each time we act, each time we speak, beginning from God and God's word, we will soon be fond of practising a spirituality that has little to do or nothing to do with God.

And so if we are going truly to live a Christian life and not just use the word 'Christian' to disguise our narcissistic and Promethean attempts at a spirituality without worshipping God and without being addressed by God, it is necessary to return to Square One and adore God and listen to God. Given our sin-damaged memories that render us vulnerable to every latest edition of journalistic spirituality, daily reorientation in the truth revealed in Jesus attested in Scripture is required. And given our ancient predisposition for reducing every scrap of divine revelation that we come across to a piece of moral/spiritual technology that we can use to get on in the world, and eventually to get on with God, we have proven time and time again that we are not to be trusted in these matters. We need to return to Square One for a fresh start as often as every morning, noon and night.

Robyn Wrigley-Carr gives us help in doing this through making accessible the prayers of great women and men from the past, including Evelyn Underhill. This *Prayer Book* enables us each day to reflect, pray and remember who we are and whose we are.

Robyn was my student for years at Regent College in Vancouver, Canada. She was a fine student who took God seriously in her life. It gives me great pleasure to encourage the reader to return to this book daily. It will help you to return to Square One.

Eugene Peterson

Introduction

Discovering the Prayer Books

In 2016, I researched the influence of Baron Friedrich von Hügel on Evelyn Underhill, working in several UK archives. I had not planned to visit the Retreat House at Pleshey (near Chelmsford), where Underhill led retreats. However, at the last minute, as a complete afterthought, I went.

In the late afternoon at the Retreat House, I discovered a dark brown, leather-bound volume. It had two bronze clasps, both engraved with a Celtic design. At first it seemed to be locked, but as I opened it I saw it contained red calligraphy headings and a collection of prayers.

Numerous Underhill scholars have alluded to the book of prayers that Underhill used for leading spiritual retreats. Margaret Cropper described 'a special book of prayers' that Underhill 'had collected which went to retreats with her, for she . . . read prayers from this special collection.'[1] In 1990, Grace Adolphsen Brame found some unpublished Underhill retreat talks that repeatedly displayed the initials, 'P.B.'. Brame assumed they referred to Underhill's *Prayer Book*, which, she lamented, 'can no longer be found . . . that little book of prayers which Underhill had made herself, one single copy of hand-written prayers which she loved . . . If that is ever found, it will be a treasure.'[2]

I wish to acknowledge the Australian Research Theology Foundation Inc. for a grant that enabled me to do this research.

And now this 'treasure' that scholars assumed lost decades before was found.

I didn't know at the time, but this was Underhill's second *Prayer Book*, dated 1929–38. The handwriting at times is quite illegible. I imagine some of the prayers were scrawled by Underhill in bed, given she stopped leading retreats in 1938, due to ill-health. So how had this *Prayer Book* suddenly re-emerged?

In 2004, the Canadian-born priest Father Bill Kirkpatrick sent this leather-bound *Prayer Book* to the House of Retreat at Pleshey. He had bought it many years earlier at an Oxfam shop and had greatly benefited from using it for his personal prayers. Kirkpatrick described it as 'full of . . . good things on the mystery we are all caught up in'.[3] I understand that the Warden at the time had placed this *Prayer Book* in a suitcase for safekeeping, where it lay, forgotten.

So, having stumbled upon this 'treasure', I began to copy out the *Prayer Book*, with a clear sense that God had set up this discovery. And as I copied, I sensed that great 'cloud of witnesses' Paul describes in Hebrews 12, in an arc above, smiling enthusiastically, cheering me on to do the work of making Underhill's *Prayer Book* accessible to a new generation.[4] For these prayers were written by lovers of God from different branches of the Church, from the third to the twentieth century. And these prayers had blessed retreatants for decades, until they were mysteriously lost.

A few months later, I returned to Pleshey to check my copied manuscript with the original. To my absolute amazement a second *Prayer Book* had also mysteriously emerged. This was the first *Prayer Book* that Underhill wrote. The yellow and blue, flowery print cover, with light-blue ribbon book mark, was most probably hand-bound by Underhill. The handwriting is much neater, indicating it as the earlier of the two *Prayer Books*. I would roughly date it as from 1924, when Underhill started taking retreats, until 1928, just before the second *Prayer Book* begins. This earlier *Prayer Book* is 67 pages, whereas the later one is nearly double, at 129 pages.[5] Both *Prayer Books* have the identical, defining feature of usually beginning a prayer with a red, decorative letter in calligraphy. Also, most pages have a heading that relates to the index at the back of each *Prayer Book*. Fifty-five prayers from the first *Prayer Book* are repeated in the second *Prayer Book*. In this edition, I have only provided the prayer in the first instance. Each page of the original *Prayer Books* had a page number for identifying prayers in the indexes. Here I have kept the original page numbers for the prayers for the first *Prayer Book* but have continued the page numbering for the second *Prayer Book* and adapted and combined the indexes into one.[6]

Having outlined the discovery, we now turn to examine two aspects of Underhill's story that are directly relevant to her *Prayer Book*: the influence of Baron Friedrich von Hügel on her choice of prayers, and Underhill's retreat leading – the context in which her *Prayer Books* were used.

Underhill's story - von Hügel's influence

I owe him [von Hügel] my whole spiritual life. (Underhill)[7]

The Catholic layman, Friedrich von Hügel (1852–1925), had a significant influence on Underhill's choice of authors in the *Prayer Book*. But first, a little of Underhill's spiritual narrative before she came under von Hügel's spiritual nurture, to provide the context for his remarkable influence upon her.

Evelyn Underhill (1875–1941) was raised in a secular home and joined an occult group, the Order of the Golden Dawn, in 1904. She was a member of this group for a few years but writes, this period 'did not last long'.[8] Underhill narrates part of her journey:

> For eight or nine years I really believed myself to be an atheist . . . Gradually the net closed in on me and I was driven nearer and nearer to Christianity, half of me wishing it were true, and half resisting violently.[9]

Eventually, after spending a few days at a convent in 1907, Underhill was 'overcome by an overpowering vision' that 'convinced' her 'that the Catholic religion was true'.[10] From that encounter, Underhill was heading for acceptance into the Roman Catholic Church, but her fiancé, Hubert, responded to this prospect with a 'storm of grief, rage and misery'.[11] Hubert's opposition, coupled with the Catholic Modernist crisis, halted Underhill's conversion.

Underhill was confirmed into the Church of England at boarding school, then, in 1921, through von Hügel's influence, she became a practising member of the Anglican Church. Though she resonated with Catholic spirituality, often worshipping in Catholic churches, Underhill stayed an Anglican her entire life.[12] Lord Ramsey, a former Archbishop of Canterbury, suggests that Underhill was one of the few in the Church of England in the 1920s and 1930s who helped people to 'grasp the priority of prayer in the Christian life and the place of the contemplative element within it'.[13] The primary influence on Underhill's grasp of these 'priorities' was von Hügel.

Underhill's life was transformed dramatically through von Hügel's spiritual direction from 1919 until 1925. Evelyn Underhill's close friend, Lucy Menzies, describes the Baron as Evelyn's 'final court of appeal in all things spiritual . . . she drank deeply of his spirit'.[14] Underhill came to the Baron drifting spiritually with an abstracted sense of the mystical life. Through von Hügel's influence, Underhill came to encounter Christ, describing this experience vividly:

> Until about five years ago I never had any personal experience of our Lord. I didn't know what it meant . . . Somehow by his prayers, or something, he [von Hügel] compelled me to experience Christ. He never said anything more about it – but I know humanly speaking he did it. It took about four months – it was like watching the sun rise very slowly – and then suddenly one knew what it was.[15]

In addition to this Christocentric influence, von Hügel encouraged Underhill to the Institutional Element.[16] He described Underhill as needing 'de-intellectualizing', having too much blood lodged in her brain.[17] He wanted to balance her intellectual focus with the institutional: care for the poor, church attendance, partaking in the Eucharist.

Von Hügel also had a profound impact on Underhill through the authors he encouraged her to read. The Baron always recommended his spiritual directees engage in 15 minutes of daily 'spiritual reading', which he described as like having 'a lozenge melt imperceptively in your mouth'.[18] The words of these spiritual writings were to be savoured and prayed, not simply read with the head and lodged in the mind. He wanted significant, spiritual insights to disperse into the bloodstream and be assimilated into the *whole* person.

Von Hügel's influence on Underhill's choice of authors in her *Prayer Books* is significant. The most obvious imprint is displayed through *The Imitation of Christ* being the text most quoted in Underhill's *Prayer Books*. This book was von Hügel's 'staple spiritual food';[19] the words he encouraged his directees to 'work into' their lives.[20] In addition, Augustine's *Confessions*[21] is quoted in Underhill's *Prayer Books*. Von Hügel tried to 'live' this book, 'at its deepest', for 50 years.[22]

Other authors that von Hügel repeatedly recommended for spiritual reading are also quoted in Underhill's *Prayer Book*. These include Pere Grou,[23] François Fénelon,[24] Francis de Sales,[25] Teresa of Avila and John of the Cross,[26] Jean Pierre de Caussade[27] and Élisabeth Leseur.[28] Underhill also includes Scripture in her *Prayer Books*, particularly the Psalms.[29] The Baron had recommended that his directees pray the psalms because of their 'richness, reality [and] penetrating spirituality'.[30]

Though we clearly recognize the Baron's influence on some of the authors that Underhill selected, she chose the specific prayers herself. Charles Williams tells us that 'each new prayer had to be on probation for some time before she admitted it to her collection'.[31]

Authors of the selected prayers

In the earlier, flowery-covered *Prayer Book* most of the prayers are quotations that Underhill selected from great men and women of prayer, through the centuries, from all branches of the Christian Church. On the back of the page, Underhill provides her own short prayers. But by the second half of the later, leather-bound *Prayer*

Book the majority of the long prayers are written by Underhill herself. Throughout the *Prayer Book*, if no author's name is stated, the prayer is written by Underhill.

Underhill's *Prayer Books* include authors from the third to the twentieth centuries, with the greatest concentration of authors from the sixteenth century. Short biographies of each author plus information about the church liturgies Underhill draws upon are provided in this volume in the section 'Author biographies and liturgical sources'. The authors included are:

Third century	Augustine
Fourth century	Ambrose
Sixth century	Pope Gregory VII
Eighth century	Alcuin of York, Rabia al-Basri
Ninth century	John Scotus Eriugena
Tenth century	Æthelwold of Winchester
Eleventh century	Anselm
Twelfth century	Francis of Assisi
Thirteenth century	Richard Rolle, John of Ruysbroeck, Thomas Aquinas
Fifteenth century	Ignatius of Loyola, Nicholas of Cusa
Sixteenth century	Teresa of Avila, Launcelot Andrewes, Pierre de Bérulle, John Donne, Frances de Chantal, John Bradford, Luis de Leon, Sir Francis Drake
Seventeenth century	Gertrude More, Bishop Thomas Ken, Jean Pierre de Caussade, Jeremy Taylor, William Law, John Eudes

Nineteenth century	John Henry Newman, Edward Pusey, Father Baker, James Martineau, Christina Rossetti, Janet Erskine Stuart, Ottokár Prohászka
Twentieth century	Margaret Cropper, Edward Keble Talbot

Only four centuries have no authors represented. As well as Anglicans, Roman Catholics and Orthodox writers, Underhill includes a Sufi mystic. The enormous diversity in Underhill's choice of liturgies also displays her eclectic, wide reading and knowledge of different branches of the Church.

In addition to prayers from historical saints, Underhill had her close friend, Sorella Maria di Campello, contribute to the *Prayer Book*, as translated at 120 (page 88–9).[32] We also have two small contributions from Underhill's friend, Marjorie Vernon, her nurse during her final years.[33]

We now turn to discuss the context for the use of these specially selected prayers.

Underhill's retreat leading

Underhill went on her first retreat at Pleshey in 1922. She recalls her 'alarm at the idea of silence, and the mysterious peace and light distilled by it' and her 'absolute distress when it ended, and clatter began'.[34] By June 1923, she would declare to Lucy Menzies, 'The retreat house I always go to is Pleshey',[35] which became '*my dear* Pleshey'.[36] For Pleshey is 'steeped . . . in centuries of prayer and adoration . . . full of Life and Light'.[37]

When asked to take a Pleshey retreat in 1924, Underhill's 'whole face lit up, and she said that to conduct a retreat was something she had longed to do'.[38] It was new for the Church of England to have a woman leading retreats and Underhill was a pioneer in this work.[39] As T. S. Eliot states, 'With shrewdness and simplicity she helped to support the spiritual life of many.'[40] For over a decade, Underhill led retreats at Pleshey and at other locations, such as Moreton, Leiston Abbey, Glastonbury and Little Compton.[41] Some years she led as many as seven or eight retreats, always with two of these at Pleshey. She used the same material for all of the retreats in one calendar year.[42] Her books in the last 15 years of her life were based on these yearly retreat talks.

At her retreats Underhill gave both addresses and meditations. A guided meditation was generally given at midday on the Saturday or Sunday. These meditations focused on a passage or event in Scripture as material for prayer.[43] Underhill's addresses were given daily at 10.00 a.m., 5.00 p.m. and 8.30 p.m. For her addresses, Underhill always had an overriding metaphor, as evident in her published retreat addresses, for example, *The House of the Soul* (1926), *The Mount of Purification* (1931), *The Light of Christ* (1932), *Abba* (1934), *The Mystery of Sacrifice* (1935) and *The Fruits of the Spirit* (1936).

Underhill usually arrived a day early to Pleshey to prepare. She placed a keynote quotation or a visual stimulus on the noticeboard in the chapel before her retreats. At the chapel porch she put up 'suggestions for Bible readings, Points for Meditation, times for interviews, the Hymn Sheet . . .'.[44] Underhill chose all the hymns and led prayers and the Eucharist at 12.30 p.m. daily. A time of rest and recreation was allowed from 2.00 p.m. until 4.30 p.m. each day. Underhill always had intercessors praying for each retreat, whose names were given on the final night.[45] Underhill preferred a small group at her retreats, so that she was able to offer 'interviews' (spiritual direction) twice daily, in the conductor's sitting room.

The *Prayer Book* was crucial to each retreat as it contained the prayers that Underhill read during times of worship in the Pleshey chapel. Underhill's *Prayer Books* were working documents as she adapted existing prayers to fit in with the themes of specific retreats. In the originals of the *Prayer Books*, we see the different fountain pens and pencils used on the same piece of text, indicating revisions and additions at different times. For example, in prayer 94, the original word is changed to 'peace', and the heading 'patience' is added, presumably to make it more suitable for Underhill's 'Fruit of the Spirit' retreat in 1935. In this publication of the *Prayer Books*, I have provided the most recent changes, stating in the notes where earlier options for particular wording are provided in the original manuscripts. The *Prayer Book* indexes were also added to gradually, as revealed through the final page of the second *Prayer Book* index being out of alphabetical order. Another observation is that Underhill did not always fill each page in a sequential way. Throughout the *Prayer Books* we find blank pages here and there, indicating that any particular page could be written upon at random.

I hope that these prayers enrich both your personal life and your involvement in corporate prayer.[46]

Robyn Wrigley-Carr

Evelyn Underhill's Book of Private Prayers[1]

1

Our Father
in heaven,
Hallowed be Your name;
Your kingdom come;
Your will be done;
In earth as it is in heaven.
Give us this day our daily bread.
And forgive us our trespasses,
As we forgive them that trespass against us.
And lead us not into temptation;
But deliver us from evil:
For Yours is the kingdom,
The power, and the glory,
For ever and ever, Amen.

Let us ask for a closer communion with our Lord.[2]

2
Communion with God

O Lord (who shall) grant unto us now to find You alone, that we may open to You our hearts and enjoy You as our souls desire. When You alone shall speak to us, and we to You, good Lord;

as one friend is accustomed to speak to another secretly. This we desire and pray Lord Jesus, that we may be fully drawn[3] to You, gathered wholly in You and utterly forgetting ourselves. That You might be with us,[4] and we with You, and thus assembled make us ever to dwell together, we pray.[5]   (*Imitation* IV.13)

3
God's love

O Lord, how great is the multitude of Your sweetness to them that fear You. But what are You to those that love You? What to them that serve You with all their hearts? The sweetness of the contemplation that You grant to those that love You is unspeakable. Here You show most fully the sweetness of Your charity: that when we were not, You made us, and when we erred from You, You led us again to serve You, and You commanded us to love You. How can we forget, since You remembered us? Even when we failed, You were merciful to Your servants, and have shown us grace and friendship above all our deserts.   (*Imitation* III.2)

Let us pray for the graces of fortitude and perseverance.

Let us ask that the healing and strength and power of God may come into our souls.

4
Grace

We bless You, heavenly Father, Father of our Lord Jesus Christ, because You remember us. When You come into our hearts, we are filled with Your joy. You are our glory, the exultation of our hearts; You are our hope and refuge in the day of trouble. But because we are feeble in love and imperfect in virtue, therefore we need to be strengthened by You. Therefore visit us, Lord, oft times; and instruct us with holy discipline. Deliver us from our evil passions and heal our hearts from all wrongful affections: that we, inwardly healed and well purified, may be able to love, strong to suffer, steady to persevere.   (*Imitation* III.6)

Let us ask for grace to do the will of God.

5
God's will

Most merciful Jesus, grant us Your grace that it may be with us and work with us and abide with us to the end. Grant us ever to do Your will and to desire that which is most acceptable to You and most dearly pleases You. May Your will be our will, and may our will ever follow Your will and agree to it in all things. Be there in us one willing and one not willing with You; and let us will nothing but what You will. Grant us for Your sake to love to be despised and unknown in the world. (Grant us, above all things, desire to rest in You and to poise our souls in You.) You are the very peace of heart; You are our only rest, without You all things are hard and unquiet. So that our wills be right and abide steadfast in You, do to us in all things that please You; for it may not be but good, whatsoever You do to us. If You will that we be in light, blessed may You be; if You will that we be in darkness, blessed may You be. Give us grace gladly to suffer for You whatever You will shall come upon us. May we indifferently receive of Your hand good and evil, bitter and sweet, glad and sorrowful; and for all things that befall us, give thanks to You. (*Imitation* III.17, 19)

6
Transformation

Make us like Yourself, O God, since in spite of ourselves, such You can make us. You have shown it to be possible in the face of the whole world by the most overwhelming proof, by taking our created nature on Yourself and exalting it to You. Let us have in our own person what in Jesus You have given to our nature. Let us be partakers of that divine nature. Enter our hearts substantially and personally, filling them with You. (J. H. Newman)

7
Protection

To You are our eyes directed, O God, Father of mercies. Bless and sanctify our souls with a heavenly blessing, that they may be Your holy habitation and nothing may be found in the temple of Your honour that may offend the eyes of Your Majesty.

Look upon us according to the greatness of Your goodness and the multitude of Your pities. Defend and keep the souls of Your little servants among so many perils of this corruptible life: and, Your grace going with us, direct us by the way of peace to the country of everlasting clearness. (*Imitation* III.64)

Let us commit ourselves to our Lord's guidance.

8
The true pilot

O Christ who are a most true pilot and guide, and also most expert, faithful and friendly, put out Your hand, open our eyes, make Your high way known to us which You first entered into. You are the way: lead us to the Father by Yourself, that we all may be one with Him as You and He together be one. Show us the way we should walk in, for we lift up our souls unto You.   (H. B., 1566)

Joy

Good Lord, give us joyfulness of heart and peace of conscience; continual gladness and consolation in Your word and promises; that we may evermore be thankful unto You and praise Your name for ever.

Let us renew our personal consecration to Our Lord.

9
O Master Christ

You have loved us with an everlasting love:
You have forgiven us, trained us, disciplined us:
You have broken us loose and laid Your commands on us:
You have set us in the thick of things and deigned to use us:
You have shown Yourself to us, fed us, guided us.
Be graciously pleased to accept and forgive our poor efforts,
And keep us Your free bond slaves for ever.

Let us ask God's help in the reordering of our lives.

10
Mortification

O God, it is true that self-subjection frightens the cowardly; who are thus because, counting on themselves, they lack confidence in You. Thus have we been until now; but we desire no longer so to be. We are resolved to attack in ourselves all that You show us to be contrary to Your love. You know the measure of love and holiness You await from each one of us; we cannot fulfil it without an equal measure of renunciation. We have made our choice; but we can do nothing without You. Help us; strengthen us. We begin very late; make up for all our wasted years. You can do it, You will to do it; it will be our fault if You do not do it, and we shall have to reproach ourselves with having failed to love You in time, and with failing to love You in eternity, as much as You desire and as we ought to do.

(J. N. Grou)

Let us ask for an increase and deepening of our faith.

11
Eriugena

God our salvation and redemption, who has given us nature, give us also grace. Manifest Your light to us, feeling after You and seeking You in the shades of ignorance. Recall us from our errors. Stretch out Your right hand to us weak ones, who cannot without You, come to You. Show Yourself to those who seek nothing beside You. Break the clouds of vain imaginations, which suffer not the eye of the mind to behold You in that way in which You permit those that long to see, though it is invisible, that face of Yours which is their rest: the end beyond which they crave for nothing, since there can be no good beyond it, which is higher than itself.

(John Scotus Eriugena)

Let us ask God to take and use us, in the world of prayer, according to His will.

12
St Teresa

Do, O Lord, so dispose according to Your will, that we Your servants may do You some service. Other women there have been, who did heroic deeds for You. Strengthen our souls and prepare them, O good of all good, ordain the means whereby we may do something for You, so that there may be not even one who can bear to receive so much, and make no payment in return.

Behold our lives, our faculties, our wills: we have given them all to You. We are Yours; dispose of us according to Your will. We see well enough, O Lord, how little we can do. But now having drawn near to You – having ascended this watchtower from which Your truth can be seen – and while You depart not from us, we can do all things.   (St Teresa of Avila)

Let us offer ourselves again for God's service and ask Him for strength in which to do it.

Let us ask for the grace of continuing faithfulness in the service of God.

13
Service

O God who has appointed for all Your children a war to wage and a kingdom to win, accept and fit us, we pray, for Your service. Enter, cleanse and inspire our hearts in this day of our visitation. Give to us the Spirit, not of fear, but of power, of love, and of discipline.[6] Lead us to the battlefields which You have prepared for us and meet us there with the comfort of Your help: that though of ourselves we can do nothing, yet by Your grace and in the fellowship of Your saints, we may minister to the needs of our generation and to the coming of Your kingdom in peace, Amen.

Lord Jesus, who stretched out Your hands of love on the hard wood of the cross that all might come within the reach of Your saving embrace: clothe us in Your Spirit, that we, stretching forth our hands in loving labour for others, may bring those who do not know You to the knowledge and love of You.

Let us ask for a renewal of the Spirit of confidence and joy.

14
Joy

Let us not seek out of You what we can find only in You, O Lord; peace and rest and joy and bliss, which abide only in Your abiding joy. Lift up our souls above the weary round of harassing thoughts to Your eternal presence. Lift up our souls to the pure, bright, serene, radiant atmosphere of Your presence, that there we may breathe freely, there repose in Your love, there be at rest from ourselves and from all things that weary us, and then return clothed[7] in Your peace to do and bear what shall please You.   (E. B. Pusey)

Veni Domine

Come Lord, and live in the souls of us Your servants, in the fullness of Your purity and Your power, in the holiness of Your Spirit, in the perfection of Your mysteries and overcome all adverse powers, in Your Spirit, to the glory of the Father.   (Pierre de Bérulle)

Let us think of the love and courage of Christ and the saints.

15
The saints

Give us light, O Lord, that contemplating the love and patience of Jesus and His saints, we may be changed into love and patience. Take from us, by the contemplation of their example, all selfishness. Take from us all softness. Take from us all delicacy and fastidiousness. Take from us all cowardice and timidity. Take from us all self-love.

Give us a share in their spirit of endurance. Give us a love of labour. Give us a love of the cross. Give us a love of hardships. Give us a spirit of courage. Give us a spirit of surrendered trust. That we may be willing to spend ourselves and to be spent for the sake of Your children, in union with Your self-giving love.

16
Love

You have said, O Lord: blest are the pure in heart, for they shall see You. O sight to be wished, desired and longed for; because once to have seen You is to have learnt all things. Nothing can bring us to this sight but love. But what love must it be? Not a sensible love or a childish love, a love that seeks itself more than the beloved. It must be an ardent love, a constant love: not worn out with labours, not daunted with any difficulties. For the soul that has set her whole love and desire on You shall never find any true satisfaction, but only in You.   (Gertrude More)

Let us ask for a renewal of the Spirit of fervour.

17
Fervour

Give to us, O Lord, that life suited to our own needs, which is stored up for us all in Him who is the life of humanity. Teach us and enable us to live the life of saints and angels. Take us out of the languor, the irritability, the sensitiveness, the incapability, the anarchy in which our souls lie, and fill them with Your fullness. Breathe on us, that the dead bones may live. Breathe on us, with that breath which infuses energy and kindles fervour.

In asking for faithfulness,[8] we ask for all that we can need and all that You can give: for it is the crown of all gifts and all virtues. In asking for faithfulness we are asking for effectual strength, consistency and perseverance: we are asking for deadness to human motives and simplicity of intention to please You: we are asking for faith, hope and charity in their most heavenly exercise. In asking for fervour we are asking for the gift of prayer, because it will be so sweet: we are asking for that loyal perception of duty which follows on yearning affection. We are asking for sanctity, peace and joy, all at once. In asking for fervour, we are asking for that which, while it implies all gifts, is that in which all signally fail. Nothing would be a trouble to us, nothing a difficulty, had we but fervour of soul. Lord, in asking for fervour we are asking for Yourself: for nothing short of You, O God, who has given Yourself wholly to us. Enter our hearts substantially and personally and fill them with fervour by filling them with You. You alone can fill our souls, and You have promised to do so. Enter into us and set us on fire, after Your pattern and likeness.

(J. H. Newman)

Let us ask for the grace of perseverance.

19
Perseverance

Grant us, O God, the strength to persevere: honesty, humility and endurance therein. So govern our desires that we may ever seek You; never be content with less than You; never decline from You from weariness, self-indulgence or indifference; never mistake the beauty of Your works for You, the perfect beauty.

When the way is too hard, give us courage. When the landscape is too fair, give us purity of sight. Give us, above all, strength to give ourselves back to You, for we know that only thus we can achieve You. And when our powers are dim and we can no longer seek You, seek us of Your infinite mercy and open our eyes on the light of Your love.

Ask for the peace of God.

20
Charity

O pure charity! Come into us, and take us into You, and so present us before our Maker. You are a cleansing fire, and a comfort endlessly lasting. You make us contemplative, heaven's gate You open, the mouths of accusers You close. You make God to be seen, and You hide a multitude of sins. We praise You, we preach You, by that which we overcome the world, by whom we joy and ascend the heavenly ladder. In Your sweetness glide into us; and we commend ourselves and all ours to You without end.   (R. Rolle)

Advent

Come, O Lord, in peace; visit us with Your salvation, that we may rejoice before You with a perfect heart.   (Monastic Breviary)

Let us offer ourselves for God's service and ask for His help.

Let us ask for our Lord's presence with us.

21
Service

O God, who are the light of the minds who know You, the life of the souls that love You and the strength of the hearts that serve You; help us so to know You that we may truly love You, so to love You that we may fully serve You, whom to serve is perfect freedom.

O blessed Jesus Christ, who bid all who carry heavy burdens to come to You, refresh us with Your presence and Your power.

Quiet our understandings and give ease to our hearts, by bringing us close to things infinite and eternal. Open to us the mind of God, that in His light we may see light. And crown Your choice of us to be Your servants, by making us springs of strength and joy to all whom we serve.

Let us ask God for the grace of a well-ordered life.

22
Ruysbroeck

Give us, O Lord, a conscience pure and undefiled; a simple and well-regulated life; a humble demeaning of ourselves; and temperance in outward things. May we restrain the ungoverned desires of nature, supplying her wants with wisdom and discretion. Ministering in the world without to all who need, in love and mercy; and in the world within, emptying ourselves of every vain imagination. Gazing inward with eyes uplifted and open to the eternal truth, inwardly abiding in simplicity and stillness and in utter peace. So shall You give to us a burning earnestness of love, a fiery flame of devotion, leaping and ascending into Your very goodness itself; a loving longing of the soul to be with You in Your eternity; a turning from all things of self into the freedom of Your will; with all the forces of the soul, gathered into the unity of the Spirit, thanking and glorifying You, loving and serving You, in everlasting remembrance.

Let us ask for the gift of pure love.

Let us ask that God's will may be done in us and through us.

23
Election

Let all creatures be silent before You; and, O my God, alone speak unto us. In You alone is all we desire to know or love. If You will that we be in light, be blessed for it; and if You will that we be in darkness, still be then blessed for it. Light and darkness, life and death, praise You the Lord. Blessed be Your holy name, that our hearts do not find rest or peace in anything that we seek or love inordinately, whilst we do not love it in You and for You only. Our desire is to live to You only. Place us therefore where You will, give us or take from us what You will; only let us live to You and with You.

Let us offer ourselves to God and ask Him to remake us according to His will.

Pray that through self-offering we may learn a deeper and wider love.

24
Dedication

O God, who is able to do all things, turn us unto You. Renew our spirits, enlighten our understandings, sanctify our wills, increase our strength of body and soul; that we may depend only on You, fear and love You above all things, and serve You fervently; and that in all our efforts and desires, we may conform ourselves to Your blessed will and pleasure.

We ask You finally to impart to us Your abundant, effectual grace, by which we may be able to begin to lead a perfect and holy life, and to serve You perfectly and thoroughly even to the end. For therefore, O God, You did give us being, that we might employ it in Your service alone.   (Fr Baker)

Oblation
Lord, when we present ourselves and our love, as all the gift we have to offer at Your altar: next to our love to You, O for the sake of Your infinite love to us, which we there remember, give us grace to love our neighbour as You have loved us, and have given Yourself for us, an offering and a sacrifice to God.   (Bishop Ken)

The eyes of all wait on You, O Lord.

Jesus said, 'I am the living bread that comes down from heaven. He that eats of this bread shall live for ever.'⁹

25
Before communion
Lord, we come unto You to the end that wealth may come unto us of Your gift, and that we may joy at the holy feast that You have made ready for us. For You are our health, our redemption, our strength, honour and joy. Our souls desire Your body, our hearts desire to be united only with You. Give Yourself to us, good Lord, and we are sufficed, for without You no consolation or comfort is good. Without You, we may not be, and without Your visitation, we may not live. O marvellous gentleness of Your unspeakable pity towards us, that You Lord God, creator and giver of life unto all spirits, have willed to come to our poor souls; and have granted

to our poor, lean and dry souls to be fed[10] with Your grace and be anointed with the holy unction of Your sweet spirit.

O right, sweet, beloved Lord, the heaven and earth and all the ornaments of them hold silence in the presence of Your face. For what praise, honour and beauty they have, it is of Your mercy and bounty; and cannot be like unto the honour and beauty of Your holy name and of Your wisdom, whereof there is no number, neither end. (*Imitation* IV.3)

Let us praise the glory of Christ.

26
Retreat

O Almighty God, whose blessed Son held communion with You in the retirement of solitary places: grant, we pray, that we, Your children, following the example He has left us, may find refreshment for our souls and strength for Your service in the silence and solitude of our retreat.

Let us ask for the graces of the purified.

27
Beatitudes

Grant, O Lord, that having put aside every weight and the sins that do so easily beset us; and every motion both of flesh and spirit which is contrary to the will of Your holiness:

We may be meek, that so we may inherit the earth:

May be peacemakers, that so we may be called children of God:

May be merciful, that so we may obtain mercy:

May be poor in spirit, that so we may have part in the kingdom
of heaven:

May be pure in heart, that so we may see God:

May hunger and thirst after righteousness, that so we may be filled:

May mourn, that so we may be comforted:

And may be prepared for persecutions and reproaches for righteousness' sake.

That so our reward may be in heaven.

(Launcelot Andrewes)

Let us ask for an increase in the heavenly gifts of faith, hope and
charity.

28
For grace

Let us find grace in Your sight, O Lord; that we may have grace to
serve You acceptably with reverence and godly fear. And let us also
have that second grace, not to receive that grace in vain, or to fall
short of it: at least in any wise not so to neglect it as to fall from it,
but to stir up and rekindle it, so as to grow in it, and abide in it, to
the end of our life.

And, O, make perfect to us that which is lacking to us in Your
gracious gifts:

Of faith, add to our little faith.
Of hope, confirm our trembling hope.
Of love, kindle its smoking flax.

Shed abroad in our hearts Your Love; that we may love You, and our friends in You, and our enemies for You.

You, who give grace unto the humble, even to us, give grace to be humble.

You, who never give up them that fear You, unite our hearts to fear Your Name; and be this fear our confidence.

(Launcelot Andrewes)

29
Benediction

The power of the Father, guide and guard us.

The wisdom of the Son, enlighten us.

The working of the Spirit, quicken us.

Guard our souls. Strengthen our bodies.

Our senses, refine; our conduct, correct; our characters, set in tune.

Bless our actions: perfect our prayers: breathe into us holy thoughts. Our sins that are past, forgive, our present sins, amend, and future sins, prevent.

Unto Him that is able to do exceeding abundantly, far beyond all that we ask or think, according to the power that works in us: to Him be glory in the Church in Christ unto all generations.[11]

(Launcelot Andrewes)

O Lord our God! Save Your people and bless their inheritance. Keep in peace Your whole Church.

30
The holy house

O Lord our God, whose might surpasses understanding, whose glory cannot be measured, whose mercy is infinite and love of all unspeakable: O Lord, in Your mercy, look down on us and on this holy house. Give to us, and those who pray with us therein, the riches of Your grace and of Your mercy. Sanctify those who love the beauty of Your house, give them in return, honour, by Your Divine power, and do not forsake us who hope in You, Lord and Master. Our God, who has established in heaven the orders and armies of angels and archangels to serve Your Majesty, grant that Your holy angels may enter with us here, and with us serve and glorify Your goodness.[12] For to You belongs all glory, honour and adoration, Father, Son and Holy Spirit, now and ever, world without end.

Let us ask for a new realization of Christ's presence in our daily lives.

31
Christ's presence

Open our eyes, O Lord, that we may learn to know You in Your humble lowliness and discover You in the sanctifying prose of daily duty. For there, You do truly dwell; it is in this simple duty, whatever may be its form, that we are sure to meet You. Lord, we are inattentive students and forgetful pupils; it is needful that You repeat to us each day the lesson of Your invisible presence. Increase our love and reverence, that at last we may learn to see You where You are: in ourselves, in our neighbours, in all the events of our life, in our labours, our burdens, our sufferings, and in every sacrifice.

(P. Charles)

Let us ask for a deepened sense of Christ's presence in our future lives.

Let us ask God to lead us in this retreat more deeply into His presence and knowledge of Himself.

32
Co-operation

Guide us, O Lord! And teach us to understand that You do not stand afar off as a task-master, but do entreat from nearby the souls that are Your own: and all are Yours, by vocation. Work together with us. Our poverty shall then be sweet and fruitful, and, having nothing of our own, we shall be altogether Yours.   (P. Charles)

Seeking God

Lord, teach us to seek You, and show Yourself to us as we seek; for we cannot seek You, unless You teach us, nor find You, unless You show Yourself. May we seek You, in longing for You, and long for You, in seeking; may we find You, in loving You, and love You, in finding.   (St Anselm)

Let us ask for an increase of patience.

33
Patience

Lord, make possible by Your grace that which seems impossible by nature. You know, Lord, that we can suffer little, and that we are soon thrown down with little adversity. Make, Lord, every trial or tribulation to us amiable and, for Your name, desirable; for to suffer and to be vexed for You is full wholesome for our souls.

(*Imitation* III.56)

Teach us, good Lord, to serve You as You deserve; to give and not to count the cost; to fight and not heed the wounds; to toil and not to seek for rest; to labour and not to ask for any reward, save that of knowing that we do Your will.   (St Ignatius Loyola)

34
Suffering

Keep us, O God, by Your grace, from all sin. But as for those sufferings which are the martyrdom of self-love, and those holy humiliations which crucify our pride, these we accept with our whole hearts; not so much as the effects of Your justice, but rather as the kindly acts of Your great mercy. Therefore, Lord, have pity on us, and help us with Your grace.   (De Caussade)

Prevenience

Lord, we lift up our hands unto Your commandments, which we have loved. Open our eyes, and we shall consider You; move our hearts, and we shall fervently desire You; order our goings, and we shall walk in the path of Your commandments. O Lord God! be our God; and beside You be there to us none other; none other person, none other thing, with You.   (Launcelot Andrewes)

Let us ask God to enlighten our minds and give us right judgement and prudence.

Let us ask that the Holy Spirit may purify us from every thought or desire that is not pleasing to God.

35
Right judgement

Grant us grace, O Lord, to know that which we need to know, to love that which should be loved, to praise that which highly pleases You, to seek[13] those things which are precious in Your sight, and to turn from[14] those things which are vile before You. Suffer us not to judge according to our unlearned humanity; but with true judgement to discern things visible and invisible, and above all things, always to search and follow Your will and pleasure.

(Imitation III.50)

Purification

Let Your good Spirit enter into our hearts, and there be heard without utterance, and, without the sound of words, speak all Truth. For Your mysteries are exceedingly[15] deep and covered with a sacred veil. Free our hearts from all that is defiling and unholy, from all vain and hurtful thoughts. Fence us roundabout with the holy and faithful guard and mighty protection of Your blessed angels, that the enemies of all good may go away ashamed.   (Roman Missal)

Let us offer ourselves to God without reserve for His service.

36
Élisabeth Leseur

O God, we are and desire to be wholly Yours, in endurance and in peace, in dryness and inward joy, in health and sickness, in life and death. We ask but one thing, the accomplishment of Your will in us and through us. We pursue and desire more and ever more to pursue one sole end, to increase Your glory, by the realization of Your designs for us. We offer ourselves to You in entire and intimate surrender, and beg You to use us, as the most common and passive tools, for the good of the souls You love, for Your service. Call us to a passive or an active life. Teach us to practise turn by turn, according to the occasion, the prayer we love, the works which are Your will. May we be austere towards ourselves and ever more gentle, courteous, kindly to others, drawing them through us to love You, and hiding from them[16] all our struggles, our prayers and our renunciations.

Let us ask God to enter with us into the silence of our retreat and show us those things He desires we should do.

37
Self-emptying

Lord Jesus, who did empty Yourself of Your eternal glory and become a little child for love of us, empty us wholly of ourselves; that we may love You truly, as You love us infinitely, and serve You faithfully, for Your love and mercies' sake.

St Augustine

Show us, O Lord, the path by which we may come to You. We have nothing but the desire; we know nothing, save that we should abandon the fleeting and the falling, and seek the unchanging and the eternal. This would we do, O Father, for this alone we know, but we know not the path by which to reach You. Show it to us clearly and fortify us for the way.

Let us make an act of faith in our Lord's presence with us.

Let us ask for the simplicity of love.

38
Nicholas of Cusa

Lord, we may not think that You could love anything more than You love us; for Your gaze never leaves us, and what we gaze on, that we love. Thus we know that You love us, for Your eyes are fixed on us, Your little servants, and Your look, Lord, is Your love. And because this, Your love, is ever with us, and Your Love is nought else but Yourself our lover, You are always with us Lord; You do not leave us alone, but in every way companion and cherish us.

Simplicity

Suffer us, O Father, to come to You. Lay Your hands on us and bless us. Take away from us for ever our own spirit and replace it by the instinct of Your divine grace. Take away from us our own will, and leave us only the desire of doing Your will. Give us that beautiful, that loveable, that sublime simplicity, which is the first and the greatest of Your gifts.   (J. N. Grou)

39
Rabia

O Lord, the stars are shining and all things take their rest; and kings have shut their doors and every lover is alone with his beloved: and here am I alone with You.

Inquietum cor nostrum[17]

Lord, we cannot escape You, nor withdraw our souls from Your embrace. Waken us, by Your grace, from our uneasy dreams, that we may turn to You in faith and love and pray: 'O God our Father, because You do love us, and because You have created us, be our guide. Lead us to You, that we may find our rest in You.'

(O. Prohászka)

Mutual charity

Pour down on us, O Lord God, the Spirit of Your love and ever preserve in the same mutual charity those whom You have fed with the same heavenly bread.   (Leonine)

Coming into His silence
let us confess to God in secret
our sins, failings, rebellions, mistakes,
and ask for forgiveness, strength and grace to reorder our lives
according to His will.

We have sinned against love by our selfishness, coldness and want of gentleness. By our uncharitable thoughts and words. We have been slack, impatient, obstinate, self-absorbed, wilful, easily offended.

We have done less for our neighbours, than we could have done. We have often forgotten You. For all this, O Lord, we beg Your forgiveness and mercy. We know we are weak. Give us the help and strength that by Your grace, our faults may be conquered.

40
Confession

O Lord, full of compassion and gracious, long suffering and plenteous in mercy – we have sinned, O Lord, against You. We have sinned against You many times and grievously.[18] We hide nothing. We offer no pretended excuses. We make confession against ourselves of all our sins.[19] Thus we have done; and You have not changed us as we deserve for our sins. What shall we say? Or what shall we answer for what we have done? We are without defence, condemned of ourselves: for You have dealt truly, we have done wrongly. And now what is our hope? Is it not Yourself, O Lord? Our earnest expectation is from You, O Father and Lover of all. Show Your wonderful mercy to us; say unto us: Your sins are forgiven. Say unto us: Your grace is sufficient.   (Launcelot Andrewes)

Let us ask for such new light as our souls can bear.

41
Light

The heaven, O Lord, is bright with the clear shining of the stars, and the earth is serene with radiant light, since You have shone upon the world from Your holy habitation. Chase then, we ask You, all darkness from our minds. Kindle our hearts with the splendour of Your grace. Enlighten our eyes with the radiance of Your brightness, that we may attain to see You for ever.

(Mozarabic)

O God, the true light of believers, the eternal glory of the just, whose light never fades and whose brightness knows no bounds, pour into our hearts the pure and serene light of Your truth, and grant us thereby to enter into Your eternity. That as after the night passed, You have caused us to see the light, so You may bid us come to that blessed and everlasting day.   (Ambrosian)

Let us ask that the peace of God may enter within with this retreat.

Let us bring our failings and errors into God's presence and ask Him to correct them.

42
For mercy

Author and Lord of never-ending kindness, who in Your gentleness and righteousness incline Your ear to all who humble themselves: have mercy on us. Disperse the tempests that assail us, and grant us the peace of Your tranquillity. That which by our own fault we have lost, give us again by Your generous mercy. Make our souls strong in the power of Your might. Heal the sickness of our hearts, and bring us back from the paths of error; that by You, who are the way, we may attain to You, who are the Life.

(Mozarabic and Gothic)

Order

Lord, set our lives in order; making us to know that which You would have us to do, and to do it in the way that we should.

(St Thomas Aquinas)

Let us offer ourselves to God and ask His blessing on our retreat.

Let us ask for the grace of humility.

43

House of prayer

O God, who invisibly contains all things, and yet for the help of all visibly shows forth the signs of Your power, let the brightness of Your mercy descend upon this house of prayer and grant that we,[20] who here invoke Your name, may feel the help of Your protection.   (Gregorian and Ambrosian)

Humility

O Christ, who has shown us the beauty of eternal peace and the duty of inseparable love, grant that we may ever think humbly of ourselves, abounding in gentleness and pity towards all. That following the example of Your humility, and imitating You in all things, we may live in You and not depart from You.

(Mozarabic)

Let us place ourselves in the hands of God and ask that He show us the path in which we should go.

44
The way

May the way by which we go to You, Lord, be safe, straight and fair, and may it attain its perfect end in You; being deflected neither by gladness[21] nor by grief.[22] That in gladness we may go thankfully, and in grief go patiently; being neither too much exalted by the one, nor cast down by the other.   (St Thomas Aquinas)

For light

O God, who enlightens every person that comes into this world, we ask You to enlighten our hearts and minds with the splendour of Your grace: that all our thoughts may be worthy and pleasing to Your Majesty, and that we may love You truly, and serve You faithfully.   (Roman Missal)

45
God's generosity

What shall we say, O God, of Your unspeakable generosity? When we flee from You, You recall us. When we return to You, You receive us. When we waver, You uphold us. Negligent, You stir us anew. You arm us in the battle, yet crown us when we triumph.[23] When we repent, You receive us, and do not remember our sin. For all this, how shall we suffice to praise You? We give You thanks for the abundance of Your goodness, begging that You will ever increase in us Your grace, and that which You have increased will preserve.   (St Thomas Aquinas)

Let us ask God to lead us (in this retreat) more deeply into the world of prayer.

46
Prayer

Teach us, O God, that silent language which says all things. Teach our souls to remain silent in Your presence; that we may adore You in the depths of our being, and await all things from You, while asking of You nothing but the accomplishment of Your will. Teach us to remain quiet under Your action and produce in our souls that deep and simple prayer which says nothing and experiences everything, which specifies nothing and includes everything. Do pray in us, that our prayer may ever tend to Your glory, and our desires and intentions may not be fixed on ourselves, but wholly directed to You.   (J. N. Grou)

Let us ask for the presence of Your Holy Spirit with us today.

47
The Holy Spirit

Trusting in Your word, O Lord, we wait for Your Spirit. Send Him forth from Your holy heaven to sanctify our hearts: to bring strength to the weak, peace to the troubled, light to our darkness, warmth to our coldness. That we all, who are gathered here in Your name, may share in the holy gifts which He bestows.

(Mozarabic)

Thanksgiving

Thanks be unto You, O God, our joy, our glory and our confidence. Thanks be unto You for all Your gifts. But do keep them safe for us; for then You will keep us safe, and Your gifts will increase and be perfected; and we shall be with You, for ever our being is Your gift.   (St Augustine)

Let us ask God to give this school of prayer[24] those gifts of which He knows our souls will have most need.[25]

Let us put our lives in the hand of God and ask Him to give us that food of which He knows we have need.

48
Abandonment

Lord, we know not what we ought to ask: You only know what we need. You love us better than we can love ourselves. Father, give Your children that which we know not how to ask. We dare not ask either for the sweet food or the bitter;[26] we simply present ourselves before You. Look upon our[27] needs, which we ourselves know not; see and do according to Your tender mercy. Give us the bread of life and the bread of sorrow.[28] We adore all Your purposes though we know them not. We offer and yield ourselves wholly to You; and would have no other desire but the accomplishment of Your will. Teach us to pray, and do Yourself pray in us.

(François Fénelon)

49
Grace

O Lord our God, grant us grace to desire You with our whole heart, that so desiring, we may find You: and so finding You, we may love You: and so loving You, may rejoice in You for ever.

(St Anselm)

The divine assistance

Give Your light,[29] O Father, to beginners in the way of prayer. Give understanding to Your little ones. Give help to those who are youthfully running their course. Give penitence to those who have been the negligent. Give fervour to the tepid. And give to us all a blessed end in You.   (Gelasian)

Let us pray for all those with whom we have ever been at variance.

50
Fraternal love

Lord, we offer You our prayers and peaceable offerings for all those who have in anything made us heavy, or hindered us or done us hurt or grief. And for all those also whom we have at any time made heavy, troubled, grieved or slandered, in word or deed, knowingly or ignorantly. You[30] forgive us altogether our sins and offences against You, and against each other. Take from our hearts, Lord, all suspicion, indignation, wrath, variance, and whatever may wound[31] charity or diminish the brotherly love that each of us should have toward[32] others. Have mercy on us who ask You; give grace to them that have need; and put us in such case that we may be worthy of Your grace and finally come to life everlasting.

(Imitation IV.9)

Let us ask for the spirit of sacrifice.

51
Sacrifice

O God, You have set us in the train of many martyrs and holy people: and given us, as author and finisher of our faith, one who offered Himself up a living and dying sacrifice. We are not our own, but Yours. Freely may we crucify our shrinking will, surrender ourselves to the uttermost claims of Your Spirit, and seek no peace but in harmony with You.   (James Martineau)

Humility

O Lord God, before whom the publican was justified, give unto Your servants humility of soul; that our looks be not proud, nor our thoughts arrogant, but that being refrained from all vanity and pride, and our affections weaned from good opinion and love of ourselves, we may ever trust in Your mercy and follow the example of our blessed master, Jesus Christ.   (Jeremy Taylor)

Let us ask that we may go out from our retreat with an increase of gentleness[33] and patience.

Let us ask God to give us a fresh knowledge of Himself.

52
Charity

Lord, grant us to love You with all our heart, mind and soul, and our neighbour for Your sake: that the grace of charity and kindly love may dwell in us, and all envy, harshness and ill will may die in us. Fill our hearts with patience,[34] kindness and compassion; that, constantly rejoicing in the happiness and good success of others, and putting away the spirit of criticism and envious thoughts, we may follow You, who are Yourself the true and perfect love.

For light

O great and glorious God, enlighten, we ask You, the dimness of our minds. Give us a right faith, a certain hope, a perfect charity: and grant that we may know You, in order that we may always, and in all things, act according to Your most holy and perfect will.

(St Francis of Assisi)

53
Pascal

Teach us, O Lord, to do little things as though they were great, because of the majesty of Christ, who does them in us and who lives our life; and to do the greatest things as though they were little, because of His omnipotence.

Epiphany

O God, whose only-begotten Son did appear in the substance of our flesh: grant that we may be inwardly formed anew in

His image and likeness, who took upon Himself our image and nature.   (Roman Missal)

Grant we ask You, Almighty God, that we on whom is shed the new light of Your Word may keep that light burning by faith in our hearts, and show it forth in all our works.   (Roman Missal)

Let us ask God to bring us today a deeper understanding[35] of His presence and His truth.

54
St Ethelwold

Lord, we ask You, open to us Your heavens and open our eyes to You; that from above, Your gifts may descend on us, and from below, our hearts look back to You. May Your treasures be laid open to us, and our minds laid open to You. Build us up in Your love, cleanse us with Your purity, enlighten us with Your wisdom. Keep us in Your mercy. Put forth Your own hand from heaven and bless each one of us here. May we feel the touch of Your hand, and receive the joy of Your Holy Spirit and abide in Your peace for evermore.

Union

Abide in us, Lord God, that we may abide in You, locked to You, spirit to Spirit, in the deep mystery of God and humanity.

(Margaret Cropper)

Let us ask that the peace of God may rule in our hearts.

Let us ask for a deeper knowledge of God.

55
Peace

O God whose kingdom[36] is peace everlasting, whose chosen reward is the gift of peace, and who has taught us that the peacemakers are Your children; make us, we ask You, children of quietness and heirs of Your peace; that all discords may vanish from among us and Your tranquillity be about us evermore.

Knowledge

Shine into our hearts, O loving Master, by the pure light of the knowledge of Yourself, and open the eyes of our minds to Your teaching; that in all things, we may both think and act according to Your good pleasure, and meditating on those things that are holy, may continually live in Your light.

(Dawn Office, Eastern Church, and Leonine)

Let us ask for our Lord's guidance.

Ask for perseverance.

56
Guidance

Guide us in Your way,[37] and following us, O Lord, so direct our minds by Your gracious presence, and watch over our footsteps that we may keep the path of righteousness; and ever going forward with hearts fixed on You, may come by the highway of faith to the country of eternal joy.   (Mozarabic)

Divine love

O God, who makes all things work together for good to them that love You, grant to our hearts an invincible power of love, and continually pour into our souls the holy desire of seeking You, that, being turned aside by no temptations, we may come at last where alone true joys may be found.

Let us make an act of faith to our Lord.

57

Christ triumphant

O Christ, end of the universe, in whom as their perfection every creature rests, You are utterly unknown to the wise of this world. Yet You, Jesus, are the master and light of all rational spirits, and to You alone they attain unto absolute truth. For You are alike the way unto truth and truth itself; You are alike the way unto the life of the intellect and that life itself; You are the revelation of the Father. For every blissful spirit beholds in You the invisible God, and is united in You to the unapproachable and immortal, in a fruition which is inexhaustible joy. Be merciful to us, and grant us to behold You, that our souls may be healed.   (Nicholas of Cusa)

Let us ask for strength to go forward.

Be good and faithful instruments of His purpose.

Let us give thanks for all that Christ has shown us of Himself in our retreat.

We[38] have seen and heard Your signs and teachings.

58
Members of Christ

We ask You, Almighty Father and Eternal God, that as You have deigned to make us living members of Jesus Christ our Lord; so[39] fed by His Spirit we may go on from strength to strength and even in this present life, be made partakers of His triumph and His joy.

Christ the way

We give You thanks, O Lord, because You have so lovingly granted to show us, and all faithful people that will follow You, the true and straight way to Your kingdom. Your holy life is our way, and by holy patience we walk to You, who are our head and king. And if You, Lord, had not gone before and showed us the way, who would have endeavoured to have followed? How many would have tarried behind if they had not seen Your blessed example gone before? We are slow and dull; what would we have been had not the light gone before us?   (*Imitation* III.18)

Let us give thanks for our knowledge of the splendour and beauty of God.

59
Margaret's prayer

O greater and yet more simple than our dreams of You, be thanked by Your creatures for Your very being; for the thing that is beyond us and yet in us, beneath us and above us.

Be thanked, because You are not only beautiful but beauty, not only good but goodness, not only true but truth.

Be blessed, O God, in Your doing and Your refraining, in Your creating and Your sustaining, in Your making and Your rest.

Quiet at the centre of movement: joy at the centre of pain; peace at the centre of strife.

Be blessed by your creatures.

He had a name written, that no one knew but He Himself.

(Margaret Cropper)

Let us ask that we may be used in the peace-giving[40] and strengthening unity of Christ in the world.

60
Prière simple

Lord, make us an instrument of Your healing peace.
Where there is hate, that we may bring love.
Where there is offence, that we may bring pardon.
Where there is discord, that we may bring union.
Where there is error, that we may bring truth.
Where there is doubt, that we may bring faith.
Where there is despair, that we may bring hope.
Where there is darkness, that we may bring light.
Where there is sadness, that we may bring joy.

O Master, make us not to seek so much
 To be consoled, as to console
 To be understood, as to understand
 To be loved, as to love.

For it is in giving that one receives.

It is in self-forgetfulness that one finds.

It is in pardoning that one is pardoned.

It is in dying that one wakes to eternal life.

(Old French)

61
Greek Post Communion

Grant, O Lord, that the ears which have heard the voice of Your songs may be closed to the voice of clamour and dispute; that the eyes which have seen Your great love may also behold Your blessed hope; that the tongues which have sung the *Sanctus* may speak the truth; that the feet which have walked in Your courts may walk in the region of light; and that the souls of all who have received Your blessed sacrament may be restored in newness of life. Glory be to You for Your unspeakable gift.   (Liturgy of Malabar)

62
Post Communion

Visit, we ask You, O Lord, Your family and keep in Your vigilant love the hearts which have been hallowed by Your sacred mysteries: that as by Your mercy they receive the healing gifts of eternal salvation, so by Your protecting power they may keep the same.   (Leonine)

O God, who are eternal salvation and blessedness beyond compare, grant, we ask You, to all Your servants, that we who have received things holy and blessed, may by You be enabled to be holy and blessed evermore.   (Gothic)

Defend, O Lord, with Your protection, those whom You satisfy with heavenly gifts: that being set free from all things hurtful, we may press onward with our whole heart, to the salvation which comes from You.   (Leonine)

Let us ask God to work in us those changes that He knows we need.

An even more complete surrender to Your will.

63
Indwelling light

Stay with us, Lord, and then we shall begin to shine as You shine; so to shine as to be a light to others. The light, O Jesus, will be all from You; none of it will be ours. It will be You who shines through us upon others. O let us thus praise You in the way You love best, by shining on all around us. Make us preach You without preaching; not by words but by example and by the catching force, the sympathetic influence of what we do, by our visible resemblance to Your saints.   (J. H. Newman)

Change

We know, O God, that we must change if we are to see Your face; none but the holy can see You. O support us as we proceed in this great, awful, happy change, with the grace of Your unchangeableness. Let us day by day be moulded upon You, and be changed from glory to glory by ever looking towards You.[41]

(J. H. Newman)

64
Before communion

O Master all-holy, we Your unworthy servants, drawing near Your sacred altar, do pray and ask that You will bless and hallow, by Your all-holy Spirit, us and those gifts that there we offer You, Your own things of Your own, in and for all. And all we who partake of the one bread and one cup, You unite with one another in the communion of one Holy Spirit, that we may find grace and mercy and all heavenly blessings with Your whole Church, and all those Your saints, who have through all ages been pleasing unto You.

(Liturgy of St Basil, adapted)

Let us ask for an increase of love and cast over all our imperfections the mantle of Your long-suffering love.

65
Indwelling love

O Lord, who has loved us and saved us, come and dwell in our hearts. Give us love, the sweetest of all gifts, which knows no enemy. Implant in our hearts pure love, born of Your love for us, that we may love others as You love us. O most loving Father, from whom flows all love, let our hearts, frozen by sun, cold to You and cold to others, be warmed by Your divine fire. So help and bless us now and evermore.   (St Anselm)

Forbearance

Pardon, we ask You, O God, all our failures of the past and give in Your spirit of gentleness so to bear and forbear that by love we may serve each other, and in each other serve You. That all together we may come at last to those joys You have prepared for all who unfeignedly love You.

Let us pray for the Spirit of forgiveness and long-suffering.

Let us ask for the gift of fraternal love.

66
Forgiveness

O Lord, because being compassed with infirmities, we oftentimes sin and ask pardon; help us to forgive as we would be forgiven, practising towards all Your patience and gentleness;[42] loving our brother or sister freely, as You freely love us.   (C. Rossetti)

Our neighbours

O great Lord of hearts, lodge our neighbours in our hearts, next to ourselves; let all our desires be for their[43] good; and let it be the subject of our joy and praise, O Love, to see Your love liberal to them, to see them abounding in Your blessings.   (Bishop Ken)

Love

O God, as Your infinite love is ever streaming in blessings on us, O let our souls be ever breathing forth love to You.   (Bishop Ken)

67
Rejoicing

Grant us, we ask You, O Lord our God, ever to rejoice in devotion to You; for our happiness is perpetual and full, if we are continually serving the author of all good.   (Leonine)

Perseverance

O God, who in Your loving kindness begin and finish all good things, look on us and have mercy on us; that we who by Your grace seek to follow the paths of Your will, may never turn aside from the way of life.   (Leonine and Gelasian)

68
Pleshey 1929–1938[44]

Since I am coming to that holy room
Where with the choir of saints for evermore
I shall be made Your music – as I come
I tune the instrument here at the door
And what I must do then, think here before.

(John Donne)

Yours, O Lord, is the greatness and the power and the glory and the victory and the majesty: for all that is in the heaven and in the earth is Yours; Yours is the kingdom, O Lord, and You are exalted as head above all . . . All things come of You and of Your own we have given You.   (1 Chronicles 29.11, 14)

Yours, O Lord, is the greatness and the power and the glory. Glory be to You, O Lord, glory be to You.

Through the tender mercy of our God, the dayspring from on high has visited us. In the morning will I order my prayer and will look up.

69

O God! give Yourself to us! Restore Yourself to us! We love You! If it be too little, let us love You with more might. Let our lives run to Your embrace and turn not away till they be hidden in the hiding-place of Your countenance, till they attain to perfect peace and breathe the breath of eternity.

O God supreme! most secret and most present, most beautiful and strong. Constant yet incomprehensible, changeless yet changing all! What can I say, my God, my life, my holy joy, and what can anyone say when they speak of You?

The house of our soul is narrow. O enlarge it, that You may enter in!

You are the only reality: we are only real in so far as we are in Your order and You in us. You are more inward to us than our most inward part and higher than our highest!

70

O God, who fills heaven and earth, ever acting, ever at rest, You who are everywhere and everywhere wholly present, who are not absent even when far off, who with Your whole being fill, yet transcend, all things. You who teach the hearts of the faithful without the din of words, teach us we pray, through Jesus Christ, our Lord.

O God! our true and highest life, by whom, through whom and in whom all things live which live truly and blessedly; by whom, through whom and in whom all good things are good and lovely; mercifully grant that Your life may be in ours for evermore, through Jesus Christ our Lord.

We return unto You, O Lord, that from their wanderings and weariness our souls may rise towards You; leaning on the things You have created and passing on to Yourself, who has made them, through Jesus Christ our Lord.   (St Augustine)

Let us ask God to show us these things which He desires that we should do.

71

Show us the road by which we shall come to You. We have nothing but the desire. We know nothing save that we should withdraw from the fleeting and falling, and seek the changeless and the eternal.

This we do, O Father, for this alone we know, but we know not the road by which to reach You. This You show us clearly and fortify us for the way.   (St Augustine)

O wonderful and mighty God, whose power and wisdom has no end, You are our Father and we love and worship You for ever and ever.

A ray from Your light has shone with our inward eye; guide us onward to the perfect light, that it may illumine us wholly. Let

Your love so stir within our hearts that we may discern You clearly, for it is the pure in heart who see You. You have set us free, You have drawn us to You; therefore, guide and perfect us for Your kingdom, through Jesus Christ our Lord.   (St Augustine)

O God, who is the light of the minds that know You, the life of the souls that love You and the strength of the wills that serve You, help us so to know You, that we may truly love You, so to love You, that we may fully serve You, whom to serve is perfect freedom: through Jesus Christ, our Lord.   (Gelasian Sacramentary)

O God! greatest and most true light, from where the light of this day does spring. O light, that lightens everyone that comes into the world: O light, that knows no night, without whom all is most dark dullness: O wisdom of the world, lighten our minds that we may only see those things that please You and be blinded to all others. Grant that we may walk in Your ways this day, and that the light of Your countenance may illumine our inmost minds and kindle our cold hearts . . . This we ask through Jesus Christ, our Lord, who taught us when we pray to say, Our Father . . . [45]

72

O God, who are the[46] light of the minds that see You, the life of the souls that love You, and the strength of the thoughts that seek You, enlarge our minds and raise the vision of our hearts, that on swift wings of prayer, our spirits may reach You, the eternal wisdom, who are from everlasting to everlasting, through Jesus Christ our Lord.   (St Augustine)

O God! from whom to turn away is to fall, to whom to turn is to rise, and in whom to abide is to stand fast for ever, guard us, we pray, now and always, here and everywhere, within and without, above, beneath and on every side, through Jesus Christ our Lord. Amen.   (St Augustine)

O wonderful and mighty God, whose power and wisdom have no end, You are our Father and we will love and worship You for ever and ever. O eternal truth and true charity and blessed eternity, almighty God, whom to know is to live, whom to serve is to reign, whom to praise is the safety and joy of the soul, in You would we live and move and have our being, through Jesus Christ our Lord.
                                                        (St Augustine)

Bestow upon us, O Lord our God, understanding to know You, diligence to seek You, wisdom to find You, and a faithfulness that may finally rest in You, through Jesus Christ our Lord.
                                                (St Thomas Aquinas)

73

O God, who has prepared for them that love You such good things as pass our understanding, pour into our hearts such love towards You that we, loving You above all things, may obtain Your promises, which exceed all that we can desire, through Jesus Christ our Lord.   (Trinity VI)

Almighty and most merciful God, the fountain of all goodness, who knows the thoughts of our hearts, we confess that we have transgressed against You. Wash us, we ask You, from the stains of our past sins and give us grace and power to put away all hurtful things: so that we may bring forth fruits in keeping with repentance.[47]

O eternal light, shine into our hearts; eternal goodness, deliver us from evil: eternal power, be our support: eternal wisdom, scatter our ignorance: eternal pity, have mercy upon us. Grant that with all our heart and mind and strength we may evermore seek Your face; and finally bring us, by Your infinite mercy, to Your holy presence, through Jesus Christ our Lord. Amen.   (Alcuin)

We await Your loving mercy, O Lord, in the midst of Your temple. Your eyes shall see the King in His glory.

Think glorious thoughts of God and serve Him with a quiet mind.
                                        (Janet Erskine Stuart)

74
We put aside all that we are: we cleave to all that God is: we will bear all that troubles us, for His glory.

O God! help us to worship You after Your mind and not after our own. Help us to forget ourselves and live only for Your glory. Help us to accept gratefully our weakness and inadequacy and forget them in adoring You.

The Lord is in His holy temple: let all the earth keep silence before Him. We will enter into Your gates with thanksgiving, O God, and into Your courts with praise. We will lift up our souls in Your name and bless You while we live.

O come, let us worship and bow down: let us kneel before the Lord our Maker. For He is our God. We are the people of His pasture and the sheep of His hand.

It is a good thing to give thanks to the Lord most High, to show forth Your loving-kindness in the morning and Your faithfulness every night.

This is the day which the Lord has made: we will rejoice and be glad in it: we laid us down in peace and slept: we awaked for the Lord sustained us. Glory be to You, O Lord!

Our help is in the name of the Lord, who has made heaven and earth: blessed be the name of the Lord, from this time forth and for evermore.

75

Almighty God, unto whom all hearts be open, all desires known and from whom no secrets are hid, cleanse the thoughts of our hearts by the inspiration of Your Holy Spirit, that we may perfectly love You and worthily magnify Your holy name, through Jesus Christ our Lord.   (Gregorian)

O Lord our God, great, eternal, wonderful in glory, who keeps covenant and promise for those that love You with their whole heart, who are the life of all, the help of those that flee unto You, the hope of those who cry unto You, cleanse us from our sins and from every thought displeasing to Your goodness, that with a pure heart and a clean mind, with perfect love and calm hope, we may venture confidently and fearlessly to pray unto You – through Jesus Christ our Lord.

In the words Jesus Christ has taught us . . .[48]

You are in us and we in You: thus assembled, make us ever to dwell together, we ask You!

Let us ask God to lead us more deeply with knowledge of Himself: into His presence.

76
Lord! teach us to seek You and show Yourself to us as we seek: for we cannot seek You, unless You teach us, nor find You, unless You show Yourself.   (St Anselm)

From morning to night, may we keep You in our hearts. Long for nothing, desire for nothing, hope for nothing, but to have all that is within us charged with Your Holy Spirit and temper. Let this be our Christianity, our Church and our religion.   (W. Law)

O God, who made the stars and turns the shadow of death into the morning, we render You, our Lord and King, the tribute of praise for this new day, for the everlasting hopes that rise within the human heart, and for the gospel, which has brought life and immortality and light.

O Lord! who has brought us through the darkness of night to the light of morning, and who (and through who), by Your Holy Spirit, illumines the darkness of ignorance and sin: we ask You of Your loving-kindness to pour Your holy light into our souls, that we may ever adore You, by whose love we were created, by whose mercy we were redeemed, and by whose providence we are governed, to the honour and glory of Your holy name.

77
The praise of the crucified[49]

You are the holy Lord God. You are God of Gods, who alone works
   marvels.
   You are strong, You are great, You are most high;
   You are almighty, You holy Father, King of heaven and earth.
You are threefold and one; Lord God of Hosts.
You are good, every good, the highest good; the Lord God, living
   and true.
You are love, charity; You are wisdom;
   You are humility.
You are patience; You are fortitude and prudence.
You are security. You are rest; You are joy and gladness.
You are justice and temperance. You are all our wealth and plenty.
You are beauty. You are gentleness;
   You are the protector. You are the keeper and defender.

78

You are our refuge and strength.
You are our faith, hope and charity.
You are our great sweetness,
You are our eternal life.
Infinite goodness, great and wonderful
Lord God Almighty:
Loving and merciful Saviour.

(St Francis)

Jesus Himself drew near and went with them: and they said to one another, 'Did not our hearts burn within us while He spoke with us in the way?'[50]

O Blessed Lord! who did companion[51] with Your disciples in the countryside of Judea,[52] be with us who have come, in answer to Your love, to be with You here. And as they constrained You, saying, 'Abide with us for it is toward evening and the day is far spent', so do we here constrain You, to abide with us here.

Come, we ask You . . .

79

O Lord Jesus Christ! Word and revelation of the eternal Father, come we ask You and take possession of our souls. So fill our minds with the thought, and our imaginations with a picture of Your love, that there may be in us no room for any thought or desire that is discordant with Your holy will. Cleanse us, we pray, of all that may make us deaf to Your call or slow to obey it, who with the Father and the Holy Spirit are one God, blessed for ever more. Amen.

(W. Ebov[53])

O God! we believe that You are here present: help us to be conscious of Your presence. You know all things: You know that we love You. Help us this day in all our work and prayer, in our whole lives, that all may be done as unto You, who are our light, our hope and our joy.

Memory of the holy name at Lauds[54]
From the rising of the sun unto the going down of the same, the Lord's Name of Jesus be praised.

V. Blessed be the Name of the Lord.

R. From this time forth for evermore.

O God, who has made the most glorious name of Your only-begotten Son, Jesus Christ, to be sweet and lovely to Your faithful people but full of terror to evil spirits: mercifully grant that all who devoutly venerate this name of Jesus upon earth, may enjoy the sweetness of holy consolation in this present world, and in the world to come may attain to the glory of everlasting bliss. Through the same.

At Vespers
Whosoever shall call upon the name of the Lord shall be saved.

V. All the earth shall worship You, O God, and shall sing of You.

R. And shall praise Your name, O Lord.

80
Acts of recollection

Let us come to God as to our Father and Creator with expectant
    faith:
Let us draw near and see
  how mightily
  how perfectly
  how mysteriously
    His love is shown to us
    His children and His creatures.

Let us come to God as to one made man for us, with expectant
    faith:
Let us draw near and see
  with what humility
  with what brave innocence
  with what generosity
    His love is shown to us
    whom He calls brethren.

Let us come to God as to our Redeemer, the Lamb that was slain,
    with expectant faith.
Let us draw near and see
  with what passion
  with what cost
  with what saintly life
    His love is shown to us

whom He sanctifies,
has redeemed.

81

Let us come to God, the Spirit, as to the flame and wind, with
   expectant faith:
Let us draw near and see
   with what power
   with what light
   with what cleansing Life
      His love is shown to us
      whom He sanctifies.

Let us come to God in His Church, the Spirit-bearing body of
   Christ, with expectant faith:
Let us draw near and see
   with what heroism
   with what selflessness
   with what joy
      His love is made known in His saints
      to whose company we are called.

Let us come unto Mount Zion, to one God who is Alpha and
   Omega, with expectant faith:
Let us draw near and see
   with what radiance
   with what holiness
   with what increasing joy

His love is triumphing over
sorrow, sin and death.

Let us ask that we may be delivered from ourselves.

Let us ask for the simplicity of love.

82
Help us to pray – pray in us.

Let us ask for such new light as our souls can bear.

83
And herein we specially remember the friends of this house and all those who by prayer and service are furthering its work to Your glory and we pray You will bless those coming here this day.

Grant, O Lord, that all those who are joined together in prayer for this house may in their common action so support and confirm one another, that they may become a complete member of Your body, sharing Your life and finding vigour in the execution of Your purposes, so that in serving this place, they may come to be a strength to Your whole kingdom![55]

84
O Lord our God, whose might surpasses understanding, whose glory cannot be measured, whose mercy is infinite and love of all people unspeakable, O Lord, in Your mercy, look down on us and on this holy house. Give to us and to all those who pray with us

here, the riches of Your grace and mercy. (O Lord our God!) Save Your people and bless Your inheritance. Keep in peace Your whole Church. (Sanctify those who love the beauty of Your house, give them in return honour, by Your divine power) and do not forsake us who hope in You. O Lord and master, our God, who has established in heaven the orders and armies of angels and archangels to serve Your Majesty, grant that Your holy angels may dwell with us here, and with us serve and glorify Your goodness.

For to You belong all glory and honour and adoration, Father, Son and Holy Spirit, now and ever, world without end, Amen.

Let us ask for the graces of humility and patience.
Let us place ourselves in the hand of God and ask Him to show us the path in which we should go.

85

O God, who are the way, the truth and the life, we want Your guidance in all that we do. Let Your wisdom counsel us, Your hand lead us, Your arm support us. Breathe into our souls holy and heavenly desires, and make us like our Saviour, that in some measure we may live here on earth as He lived, and do in all things as He would have done. Amen.

86

O give thanks unto the Lord for He is gracious and His mercy endures for ever. I will magnify You, O God my King. I will praise Your name for ever and ever. Every day will I give thanks unto You and praise Your name.

God! the pastor and ruler of Your faithful servants, look down in Your mercy upon Your servant Henry, our Bishop[56] to whom You have given charge over this diocese to ever more guide, defend, comfort and sanctify, and save him and grant him by Your grace, so to advance in word and example, that he, with the flock committed to him, may attain to everlasting life, through Jesus Christ our Lord.

Almighty and everlasting God, who governs all things in heaven and earth, mercifully hear the supplications of us, Your servants, and grant unto this county all things needful for its spiritual welfare. Strengthen and confirm the faithful, protect and guide the children, visit, relieve the sick and afflicted, unemployed, those in any kind of trouble or distress, train and soften the wicked, arouse the careless, recover the fallen, restore the penitent, remove all hindrances to the advancement of Your truth and bring all to be of one heart and mind within the fold of Your holy Church, to the honour and glory of Your blessed Son, Jesus Christ our Lord.

Almighty and everlasting God, from whom comes wisdom and understanding, be present we humbly ask You, with Your servants about to deliberate in conference upon three things that matter for the maintenance, well-being and extension of Your Church in this diocese: and grant that they, seeking only Your honour and glory, may be guided in all their consultations and perceive the more excellent way and may have grace and strength to follow the same, through Jesus Christ our Lord.

87

O Jesus Christ, Lord of all good life, who has called us now Your servants to build the city of God, enrich and purify our[57] lives and deepen us in our discipleship. Help us daily to know more of You, and through us, by the power of Your Spirit, show forth Yourself to other people. Make us humble, courageous and loving: make us ready for adventure. We do not ask that You will keep us safe, but that You will keep us loyal and heroic. You, who for us faced death unafraid, and live and reign for ever and ever.

O Lord! who has set before us the great hope that Your kingdom shall come on earth, and has taught us to pray for its coming, make us ever ready to thank You for the signs of its dawning, and to pray and work for that perfect day when Your will shall be done on earth, as it is in heaven. We thank You for the work of Your Holy Spirit, within and beyond the bounds of Your Church, and we praise and glorify Your name, for ever and ever.   (87.1)[58]

Let us ask God to lead us more deeply into the world of prayer.

88
For light

O God! who enlightens every person that comes into this world, we ask You to enlighten our hearts and minds with the splendour of Your grace: that all our thoughts and works may be worthy and pleasing to Your Majesty and that we may love You truly and serve You faithfully.

89
The divine assistance

Give perfection, O Father, to beginners in the way of prayer. Give understanding to Your little ones. Give help to those who are faithfully running their course. Give penitence to those who have been negligent. Give fervour to the tepid. And give to all a blessed end in You.   (Galesian Sacramentary)

Let us ask God to find us those gifts which He knows we most need.

Let us pray for all those with whom we have ever been at variance.

Let us ask for the spirit of sacrifice.

90
Humility

O Lord God! before whom the publican was justified, give unto Your servants humility of soul; that our looks be not proud, nor our thoughts arrogant, but that, being refrained from vanity and pride, and our affections weaned from good opinion and love of ourselves, we may ever trust in Your mercy and follow the example of our blessed master, Jesus Christ.   (Jeremy Taylor)

Let us ask for an increase of charity – in all the world.

O send out Your light and Your truth, that they may lead me and bring me unto Your holy hill and Your dwelling.

Let us ask God to give us fresh knowledge of Himself.

Let us ask God to bring us into a deeper realization of His presence and His truth.

91

O Lord Christ! who in this difficult world was tempted in all things as we are – yet fell into no sin – look pitifully, we pray, upon us. Guide us with Your adorable wisdom. Teach us in everything and in every hour what we ought to do. You alone know all our life. You alone know both what we suffer and what we need. To You that perfect path which we should realize is known. Show it to us and teach us how to walk in it. Keep us, O Saviour, in body, mind and spirit; for with Your strong and gentle hands, we commit ourselves.

92

Make all those who shall come here. Bestow upon this house of prayer Your Spirit of tranquillity.

Let us ask for a deeper knowledge of God.

O Christ our Saviour! who lightened this dark world by ascending the holy cross: recharge and lighten both our souls and bodies with Your light. Let us ask Christ to teach us that which we should know.

93

Let us ask Christ[59] for a greater power of faith. That we also may seek and find many he sought and found.

Let us ask for a greater generosity of love.

94
Divine love

O God! who makes all things work together for good to them that love You, grant to our hearts an invincible power of courage and love; and continually pour into our souls the holy desire of seeking You, that being turned aside by no temptations, obstacles and hindrances, we may come at last, where alone true peace[60] is to be found.

Let us ask for strength to go forward.

Patience
Let us give thanks for all that Christ has shown us of Himself.

95
Let us give thanks for our communions.

O Christ! who under a wonderful sacrament host left unto us perpetually a memorial to Your Passion; grant us, we ask You, so to reverence the sacred mysteries of Your body and word, that we may ever feel within ourselves, the fruit of Your redemption – who lives and reigns with the Father and the Holy Spirit, one God, world without end. Amen.

Be present in our souls, O Lord, unto us, we ask You, and as You gave us an example by washing the feet of the disciples and wiping them free from all outward stain, so grant us grace ever to serve You and one another in true humility and grant that we also may have the inward stain of all our sins washed clean by You – who lives and reigns with the Father in the unity of the Holy Spirit, ever one God, world without end. Amen.

96
Post Communion
Let us pray for light.

Let us ask God to work in us those changes that He knows we need.

97
Let us go now even unto Bethlehem.

Christmas
Grant, O Lord, that the birth of Christ in us may be such that Christ's very spirit may come and take possession of our souls, all our faculties and powers, and be wholly united with us for ever – not fleetingly, but abidingly and with a settled peace (in like manner as the soul reposes in the body). Thus let us come to Bethlehem and ask the child Jesus to make His abode in us for evermore.

(Luis de Leon)

O Lord Jesus Christ! when You came to this earth, there was no room in the inn; grant to us, Your children that You may never be crowded out of our lives, but that You may find in us a dwelling prepared for Yourself.

Even so, come Lord Jesus!

98
The divine carpenter

O Lord Jesus! the master carpenter, who at the last, through wood and nails, purchased our whole salvation, wield well Your tools in our souls, these workshops, that we, who come rough-hewn, may be fashioned to a truer beauty by Your hand.

Let us ask that we may be used in the purifying and strengthening ministry of Christ in the world.

99

Let us ask that we may be transformed by the Holy Spirit into the likeness of Jesus Christ.

100

O Eternal God! who has shown to us Your glory in the face of Jesus
    Christ, our blessed Lord,
grant that we, as mirrors reflecting that same glory,
may be transformed by Your Holy Spirit, into His likeness,
and that going from glory to glory, we may at length,
in the fellowship of Your saints and holy apostles,
see and serve Him face to face,
who with You, in the unity of the Holy Spirit,

lives and reigns for ever,
Amen.

(E. K. Talbot)

101

Almighty and eternal God, from whose presence the angels go forth to do Your will: grant unto us that in obedience we may serve to the glory of Your name and, overshadowed by Your protection, receive at last the crown of life, through Jesus Christ our Lord.[61]

Let us ask for the deep peace of God in our hearts: ask Him to help us and keep it there, in spite of all surface turmoil.

102

Eternal God, in whose perfect kingdom no sword is drawn, but the sword of righteousness, and no strength known, but the strength of love: we ask You so mightily, to shed and spread abroad Your Spirit, that all peoples and ranks may be fathered under the one banner of the Prince of Peace: as children of one God and Father of all: to whom be dominion and glory, now and for ever, Amen.

Let us ask for God's guidance and protection in our meditation, our prayers and our whole lives.

103

Let us ask for a closer communion with our Lord – therefore a greater forgetting of ourselves.

Let us offer ourselves to God and ask Him to remake us according to His will.

Let us ask our Lord to teach us what we should know.

Teach us, O Lord! not to rest in this life,
But to watch, to expect, to love, as those who look for the morning:
> Inspire us to feed our lambs,
> To use our talents,
> To spend our love,
For beyond us are the hills of God, the snowfields of the Spirit, the other kingdom.

Lord! let our lives show plainly that we seek a country,
That we have a part in its triumph, though now we know only a part.
That with all Your saints and angels, we may rejoice:
That with them we may be absorbed into the ocean of divine charity.

O God! who by the lives of those who love You refashion our souls,
We give You thanks for the ministry of Your saints;
In whose lives and words Your love and majesty were made known to us,
Whose loving spirits set our spirits on fire,
Who learnt from You, the Shepherd's care for Your sheep.
Grant that some measure of the Spirit they received from You
May fall on us who love them.
> We ask it for Your own name's sake, Amen.

104

O God, who orders the common things of the common day, dignify with Your presence and help the trivial round and the routine tasks of Your servants, whose hope is in You, that our least duties may be grandly done and all activities be marked with the zeal of Your righteousness, through Jesus Christ our Lord.

O Father of love! who caused Your light to shine most brightly[62] in the darkest night of all, in the face of Jesus Christ, who, on the eve of His betrayal, gave of His best to a world that gave its worst to Him, grant us so to follow that pure light which we have seen, that more and more we may be changed into the likeness of His beauty, who with You and the Holy Spirit, live and reign . . .

For missionaries

O divine wayfarers! whose first shelter was a stable, whose first journey was a flight for life, who, travelling often, had nowhere to lay Your head, be to those who carry Your message, a sure guide and unfailing rest. Clothe them in the garment of charity which is strange and no one to teach them the language of sympathy which is understood by all, that, while strangers in every land, they may yet be welcomed as citizens of the soul of humanity, and as brethren of the human heart, for Your kingdom's sake.

St Francis

O God! who ever delights to reveal Yourself to the childlike and lowly of heart; grant, we ask You, that after the example of blessed Francis, we may learn to count the wisdom of this world as foolishness and only to know Jesus Christ and Him crucified – who lives and reigns . . .

Almighty God! who inflamed the heart of blessed Francis with a wonderful love of holy priests and a burning zeal for souls, grant that Your servant, following the example of this glorious saint, may for evermore joyfully serve You in humility and love.

105[63]
Prayer before setting out the altar vessels

O God, most pure and holy, who caused angels to watch the place where You lay in the tomb, purify me wholly, and teach me loving awe and holy fear as I touch these sacred vessels and make them ready to contain Your precious body and blood.

Let us ask for the gift of pure love:
That God's will may be done in us and through us.

106
Renew me[64]

Your compassions fail not:
They are new every morning
They that wait upon the Lord shall renew their strength;
They shall mount up with wings as eagles,
They shall run and not be weary,
They shall walk and not faint.[65]

Therefore, we pray,
   Renew us;

Renew our spirits within us;
Renew our relationships; our work; our
    capacities and gifts; our strength.
Renew our prayer.
Teach us our new song, our new name.
That we may put on the new humanity, which after
God is created in righteousness and true holiness.
For if anyone be in Christ, they are a new creature:[66]
Old things are passed away.
Behold all things are become new.
So shall You put a new song into our mouth,[67]
    Ever a thanksgiving unto our God.

(Margaret Cropper)

107
Right judgement
Let us ask God to enlighten our minds and give us right judgement
and prudence.

108
As watchmen look for the morning, so do we look for You, O
Christ.[68] Come enter the dawning day and make Yourself known to
us in the breaking of bread. For You are our God for ever and ever.

Grant, O Lord, that we who are Your soldiers here may enjoy
Your peace hereafter: that the eyes which have looked upon You
in Your sacrament of love, may also behold the fruition of Your
blessed life, that the tongues which have sung Your praises,[69] may

also speak the truth; that the feet which have stood in Your sanctuary, may walk in the land of light, and that the bodies which have been fed by Your body, may be restored to newness of life, to dwell with You, where You reign with the Father and the Holy Spirit in the unity of the Godhead, King for evermore, Amen.

(Liturgy of Malabar)

Let us renew our personal consecration to our Lord.

109

Heart of Jesus, think of me[70]
Eyes of Jesus, look on me
Hands of Jesus, bless me
Arms of Jesus, enfold me
Feet of Jesus, guide me
Body of Jesus, feed me
Blood of Jesus, strengthen me.

110

Soul of Christ, sanctify me!
Body of Christ, save me!
Blood of Christ, redeem me!
Water from the side of Christ, wash me!
Passion of Christ, strengthen me!

O good Jesus, hear me!
Within Your wounds, hide me!
Suffer me not to be separated from You!
From the malicious enemy, defend me!

In the hour of my death, call me
And bid me come unto You:
That with Your saints, I may praise You
     For ever and ever, Amen.

111
Steadfastness

Set free, O Lord, the souls of Your servants from all restlessness and anxiety: give us that peace and power which flow from You, and keep us in all perplexities and grief from any fear or faithlessness, that so upheld by Your strength, and stayed on the rock of Your faithfulness, through storm and stress, we may abide in You.

The cross

Almighty God, who has shown us in the life and teaching of Your Son the true way of blessedness, You have also shown us in His suffering and death that the path of love may lead to the cross, and the reward of faithfulness may be a crown of thorns. Give us grace to learn these hard lessons. May we take up our cross and follow Christ in the strength of patience and the constancy of faith: and may we have such fellowship with Him in His sorrow, that we may know the secret of His strength and peace, and see even in our darkest hour of trial and anguish, the shining of the eternal light.

112
Veni Creator Spiritus

Come Holy Spirit, our souls inspire
And lighten with celestial fire;

You, the anointing Spirit are,
Who does Your sevenfold gifts impart.

Your blessed action from above
To comfort, life, and fire of love;
Enable with perpetual light
The dullness of our blinded sight.

Anoint and cheer our soiled face
With the abundance of Your grace;
Keep far our foes, give peace at home:
Where You are guide, no ill can come.

Teach us to know the Father, Son
And You of both, and He but one;
That through the ages all along
This may be our endless song,
Praise to Your eternal might,
Father, Son and Holy Spirit.

Come, O Christ, into my heart, in the fullness of Your goodness. Destroy in me all that displeases You. Work in me all that
You desire, for Your glory. Come to me in the holiness of Your
Spirit. Detach me from everything which is not Yourself, to unite
me perfectly with You, and lead me to holiness in all my actions.
Accomplish in me, whatever may be the price, all Your designs, and
lead me in the narrow ways of Your pure love.

(St John Eudes)

113
Jesus our master

You meet us while we walk in the way and long to reach the heavenly country: that, following Your light, we may keep the way of righteousness and never wander away with the horrible darkness of this world's night, while You, who are the way, the truth and the life, are shining within us.

Wherever Your glory is best served, wherever and however, there and then and in that state, let us Your children be; only hide not from us Your sweet mercy and love, and teach us to trust You to the uttermost, for Your love and mercy's sake, and I come.

(F. de Chantal)

Let us ask for the presence of the Holy Spirit with us in our prayer, in our work, in our whole lives to bring strength to the weak, peace to the troubled, light to our darkness, warmth to our coldness.

114
Thanksgiving

We thank You, O heavenly Father, for all the blessings You have given: for the glory of the earth and the sky and the sea: for the sun's daily benediction and for the bright splendour of the moon and stars, and for the birds' joyful singing: for health and strength: for our friends and the friends of this house whom we remember before You: for our prayer and communion together and for Your presence in our midst. Be with us still, O Lord. Reveal to us

Your love and mercy in the days to come, and bring us all together at the last in Your heavenly kingdom, for Jesus Christ's sake, Amen.

Let us ask our Lord to take us and use us for His purposes.

O God,[71] most pure and holy, who caused angels to watch the place where You lay in the tomb; purify me wholly and teach me loving awe and holy fear as I touch these sacred vessels and make them ready to receive Your precious body and blood.

115
Grace transforming

Lord Jesus! true vine of heaven, who has promised to those that truly abide in You that they shall bring forth fruit and yet more fruit, grant that we may ever abide closely in You and receive Your promises. Help us to take from You the lifeless things of the world, and by Your transforming grace to make them part of Your eternal life. Prosper our work in all its varied efforts, You who have made us and endowed us, taught us and reproved us, redeemed us and blessed us, into this present hour. Thanks and praise, faith and adoration be unto You, for ever and ever, Amen.

Dedication
O GOD!
You have a work for me to do:
O Lord, show it to me.
You have a place for me to fill;
Give me peace to fill it to Your glory.

You have given me a soul to make:
Make it for me and build it into Your temple:
For Jesus' sake.

116

May Your overshadowing and indwelling Spirit, O God, be present
to us in this holy place: and increase in us the gifts of that Spirit,
especially that love, joy and peace which come only from You.

O King of Kings, who was invested with the royal dignity by bitter
humbling and a crown of thorns, train us and the faithful in the
fellowship of Your sufferings, that we may follow on to Your glory.

O Holy Spirit of God, from whom alone proceeds the fullness of
wisdom and life, descend, we ask You, in new glory and power
upon Your Church and the hearts of all, and bring to the world
a new birth and righteousness, new interpretations of truth and a
new wonder of love, through Jesus Christ our Lord.[72]

117

Lord! support us all day long of this thankless life until the shadows
lengthen, and the evening comes, and the busy world is hushed,
and the fever of life is over, and our work is done. Then in Your
mercy, grant us a safe lodging and a holy rest and peace at the last,
through Jesus Christ our Lord.[73]

118

Almighty Father, who in Your divine mercy covers the earth with
a curtain of darkness, that all the weary may rest; forgive the

despoiling of Your Divine Ransom[74] and grant to us and to all people, whatsoever their outward cries, rest in You this night. Let Your grace, we ask You, comfort and support all who are to spend it in sorrow, sickness, in affliction or in fear, danger, in sleeplessness, war, persecution, separation from those they love. We commend into Your hands ourselves and all those who are dear to us, all who need and seek our prayers, all who are praying for us and for this house.

Watch, dear Lord, with those who wake or watch or weep tonight, and give Your angels charge of those who sleep.

Tend Your sick ones, Lord Christ; rest Your weary ones; shield Your joyous ones; succour Your tempted ones; receive Your dying ones: for Your love and mercy's sake, Amen.

119
Passion

O Lord Jesus! who in the garden persevered in Your prayer till the victory was won: grant that in all trials and temptations, we may have recourse to You in prayer, and, resigning ourselves utterly to Your will, may endure to the end – to the glory of Your grace, who with the Father and the Holy Spirit live and reign, one God for evermore.

Are you able to drink the cup that I drink of? Lord! we know not! We dare not answer for ourselves! This only we know: that we owe ourselves to You! We are not our own. We are bought by the price of Your blood. One thing only we dare to ask for as the vision of Your cross comes before us, whatever be our past sins and our present weakness, as we kneel here with our hearts open to You. You know, Lord, we love You!

120[75]
Evening

Before the light fades, we pray, O Creator of all things, that you watch over our safekeeping.

Repel the nightmares and phantasms of the night, and restrain the enemy, so that our bodies may not be stained. Amen.

Lord, remain with us, as it is evening, and the day has already gone down.

Be present, we pray, Lord, to *Eremo* and the habitations of our dear ones, and defend them from all the pitfalls of the enemy, your holy angels dwell with us and keep us in peace. Your blessings be ever upon us. Amen.

At curfew
Good night, Mary,
My sweet hope,
I await you at the hour of my death.
Give my greetings to Jesus,
And bless my family,
And to the people of my country,
So may it be.

Eremo, grace

Father, bless the food which you provide for your poor ones, and make it so that we take it with joy and simplicity of heart to keep us united, strong and faithful in your service.

(Sorella Maria of Campello)

121

Most gracious Father! we commend to Your merciful protection all who are fighting against the enemy, or preparing to do so: all who are watching for our safety in lonely places; all air-raid wardens, engaged upon their duties; all workers supplying our needs by night and day: all who are waiting anxiously for news of loved ones; all who are wounded or are prisoners of war – all who have laid down their lives for us. May Your presence be with them and Your blessing upon them, now and always, through Jesus Christ our Lord, Amen.

Sir Francis Drake's prayer

O Lord God! when You give to Your servants to endeavour any great matter, grant us also to know that it is not the beginning but the continuing of the same, until it be thoroughly finished, which yields the true glory.

122

O great Creator of all things; who made humanity in Your own image, and through Your only-begotten Son has endowed us with the power of the Holy Spirit, to enable us to live the life of obedience to Your laws: by which alone we can claim Your promised blessings – look down, O God of mercy, upon the confusion of the world. May Your mighty Spirit infuse the truth of Your eternal Fatherhood and the community of the human race; that we may all live up to our high and glorious calling, with more faith, hope, love, courage, wisdom and service. We ask this in the name of Him who obeyed Your will, even to death on the cross, Amen.

123

O Holy Spirit of God! we ask You to quicken our minds and hearts during these days of quiet. Grant that we may see ourselves as we are, and also as You would have us to be. And give us such a vision of God our Father, as revealed to us by Jesus Christ, that we may be more completely devoted to Him, more faithful in His service, and more earnest in our endeavour to do always the things that please Him, for the sake of Jesus Christ our Lord.

O Lord Jesus Christ! Most blessed Lord! in whom is no variableness, neither shadow of turning, whose stillness is around and within us, the repose in the recollection of whose presence is joy and refreshment, enfold us in this ineffable peace, which is Your own unchanging will. Still our irritation. Soothe our restlessness: say to our hearts 'Peace be still.' Brood over us, within us, Spirit of perfect peace, so that outwardly we may reflect the inner stillness of our souls, and that we may bear change, anxiety, distractions, strains, disappointments, temptations and suffering and still be found confidently and peacefully in Your heart, O Jesus, enfolded in Your loving care. Let us[76] in true quietness, fulfil the calling which is set before us. Be it even so, dear Lord, Amen.

124

Almighty everlasting God, have mercy on Your children who are coming here to seek You. Bless the conductor. Strengthen, inspire and speak through the conductor. Help the conductor to interpret Your will to us and bless each retreatant and the gift each brings to the whole. Bless all who are praying for this retreat. Bless us who are working for it, that all may be done to Your glory. O God, we ask You to keep these Your children continually under Your protection, and direct them according to Your gracious favour, in the way of everlasting salvation – that they may desire such things as please You and, with all their strength, perform the same. And for as much as they trust in Your mercy, grant, O Lord, and graciously to assist them with Your heavenly help, that they may ever diligently serve You and by no temptation be separated from You.

O blessed Jesus! who came to seek and to save that which was lost, pour forth, we ask You, upon us, Your servants gathered together in Your name, the Spirit of Your own boundless love for souls, that they, through Your grace, may be enabled with whole hearts to dedicate themselves afresh to work for You – who lives and reigns with the Father and the Holy Spirit, ever one God, world without end.

O Lord Jesus! so dwell with them here, that they may go forth with the light of hope in their eyes, the fire of inspiration on their lips, Your word on their tongues, and Your love in their hearts. Give them, O Lord, such wisdom, sympathy and self-denial and joy, that they may draw others to You, and hereafter be partakers of Your glory, who with the Father and the Holy Spirit, lives and reigns, world without end, Amen.

We humbly ask You, O God, the Father almighty on behalf of this house: that it may please You to bless[77] and hallow all who come here and fill them with Your goodness. Let everything that is contrary to Your will be drawn out, by the power of Your Son, our Lord Jesus Christ. Your peace and joy be given to all who assemble here to worship and adore You, to all who work here for You in working for Your friends, and may Your Majesty ever protect and preserve them, O Almighty God, who lives and reigns throughout all ages, world without end, Amen.

125
Retreat

O Lord Jesus Christ! who said to Your disciples, 'Come apart and rest a while': grant we ask You to Your servants now gathered together, so to seek You whom our souls desire to love, that we may both find You and be found by You – and grant such love and such wisdom to accompany the words which shall be spoken in Your name, that they may not fall to the ground, but may be helpful in leading onward to Your perfect service, who lives and reigns, God for ever and ever, Amen.

O almighty God, whose blessed Son held communion with You in the retirement of solitary places: grant, we pray, that those who come here, following the example He has left us, may find refreshment for their souls and strength for Your service in the silence and solitude of their retreat. Grant above all, O Lord, that they may so seek You, whom their souls desire and love, that they may both find You and be found by You.

O God! master of humanity, whom to see is to love, and whom to know is life eternal, in Your life we see all those things which we fain would be. Draw near to Your servants who have come here to be near You. May the influence of Your gracious Spirit be with them, enabling them to surrender themselves to Your love and service. And when they go away from here, may the vision not fade, the loyalty not slacken. Abide with them always, that they may grow daily into the likeness of Your Spirit.

Almighty God! Father of all mercies, and giver of all comfort, deal graciously, we pray, with those who mourn, that casting every care on You, they may know the consolation of Your love, through Jesus Christ our Lord, Amen.

God! who is everywhere present, look down in Your mercy upon our friends and relations who are absent from us. Give Your holy angels charge over them and grant that they may be kept safe in body, soul and spirit and presented faultless before the presence of Your glory with exceeding joy, through Jesus Christ.[78]

May Your overshadowing and indwelling Spirit, O God, be present to us in this holy place: and increase in us the gifts of that Spirit, especially that love and joy and peace which come only from You.

126

Almighty Father, we commend to You all whom we love. Let Your fatherly hand be over them, let the great love of our Lord Jesus Christ purify their lives and inflame them with devotion to You. Let Your Holy Spirit ever be with them and so lead them in the knowledge of and obedience to Your word, that in the end they may obtain everlasting life. Have mercy upon all people for the sake of the crucified and risen Lord, who now with You and the Holy Spirit live and reign, ever one Lord, world without end. Amen.[79]

O Lord, we come to You to entreat You for others, for those who have asked us to have them in remembrance in our prayers. We are not worthy to ask of You for our necessities, yet we ask You for them. For it is You who have commanded us to pray for one another. Our master Christ, who ever makes intercession for us, has taught us to pray to You in His name. For His sake and through His intercession, we ask You to hear us for these things and people and causes, which we would now silently hold up before You in our hearts, offering ourselves for them, that You would accept us, a living sacrifice. Hear us, we ask You O Lord, and if it seems good to You, answer our prayers for others.

Bless O Lord, all those who have supported and accompanied us by their prayers in this retreat. May Your strength be with them in all their difficulties, Your light in all their times of darkness and give to them in abundance Your spirit of tranquillity and joy.

Almighty and everlasting God, who though the heaven of heavens cannot contain You, and much less a house made with hands, yet You promised to be present where two or three are gathered together in Your name: accept, we ask You, this our bounden duty and service, because holiness becomes Your house for ever, and sanctify with Your gracious presence this house, which is built to Your honour and glory. Let Your eyes be open towards it night and day. Let Your ears be so clued to the prayers of Your children. Let Your heart delight and dwell here perpetually, through Jesus Christ our Lord.

O God! before whose altar there is neither far nor near, but one eternal presence, we commend to Your gracious keeping all everywhere, whom You have united in bonds of love and worship, asking that as we pray for them, they may also pray for us, and that may maintain them and us in holy and blessed fellowship, through Jesus Christ our Lord, Amen.

127

O God our Father, who makes humanity to dwell together in families, visit, we ask, this house of prayer. Let Your holy angels dwell in it to preserve us in peace. Bless founders and benefactors of this house, all who work for it in prayer. Bless all who come here to seek You and, of Your goodness, continue the blessings You have showered on this Your house. O Lord, dwell in the midst of us and grant in Your mercy that those who seek You here may truly find You. May they be refreshed and strengthened in spirit, as well as in mind and body.

For ourselves, who are privileged to serve in Your house, we ask that You give us grace and insight, that those who come here may be hindered by nothing in us, or in our work, from finding Your peace, which is above all understanding, but that we may serve You in them. Help us utterly to forget ourselves and to give ourselves utterly to You, asking only that You use us to the full. And may Your blessing rest upon this house, on all who come to it, all who go forth from it. We ask it for Christ's sake.

Let us ask for our Lord's presence with us.

Let us ask that the Spirit of Christ may dwell in us.

Help them to come into Your nearer presence and there to abide in peace with You.

128

Grant us, O Lord, the royalty of inward happiness and the serenity which comes from living close to You. Daily renew in us the sense of joy that we may bear about us the infection of a good courage and meet all life's ills and accidents with gallant and high-hearted happiness, giving You thanks always and for all things.

O blessed Jesus Christ, who bid all who carry heavy burdens to come to You, refresh us with Your presence and Your power. Quiet our understanding and give ease to our hearts by bringing us close to things infinite and eternal. Open to us the mind of God, that in His light we may see light. And crown Your choice of us to be Your servants, by making us springs of strength and joy to all whom we serve.

For the chapel

O Lord Jesus Christ! who are the temple of the holy city of God, the light thereof and its surpassing glory, glorify and lighten, we ask You, with Your perpetual presence this earthly house, built for Your glory; and be pleased both to inspire and accept its worship day by day, the praise of thankful lives, the prayer of faithful hearts, who live and reign with the Father and the Holy Spirit. One God for ever and ever, Amen.   (Friends of Pleshey)

O God! who has filled the earth with the glory of Your presence, and led Your servants of old to make this place Your dwelling place, grant that Your children who come within its influence, may ever find You here: and going away from here may truly take You with them and return to You here again in due season. May we and they so build up our lives in You that they also may be places wherein Your Spirit dwells, filled with that strength and beauty which only comes from You, through Jesus Christ our Lord.

129

Come right in and cleanse[80] our souls by Your shining purity. Give us the energy and strength to order our souls by Your power, as You desire, and help us always to remember that everything we do is done for You and that the humblest tasks are thus glorified by Your radiance.

Almighty God, the giver of all good things, without whose help all labour is insufficient and without whose grace all wisdom is folly, grant, we ask you, that[81] Your Holy Spirit may not be withheld from this retreat,[82] but that it may promote[83] Your glory and the coming of Your kingdom. Grant this, O Lord, for the sake of Jesus Christ.

Remember what You have wrought in us and not what we deserve, and as You have called us to Your service, make us worthy of our calling, we ask You, for the sake of our Lord, Jesus Christ.

Let us offer ourselves again for God's service and ask Him for strength in which to do it.

Let us ask for the peace of continuing faithfulness in the service of God.

Let us offer ourselves without reserve to God for His service.

Élisabeth Leseur

130

Let us offer ourselves to God and ask Him to re-make us according to His will.

O God, most pure and holy,
who caused angels to watch the place where You lay in the tomb.

131

O blessed Lord Jesus Christ, who bid Your disciples stand with their loins gird and their lamps burning, be with us at this hour. Here we dedicate ourselves to You anew. Help us to run the race that is set before us with redoubled vigour and fresh vision. Teach us how to trim our lamps that they may not burn dim. Guide us to the constant recollection that the candle of the Lord is the Spirit of humanity. And by Your risen power, make us a power for You in this place[84] for Your own name's sake.

132

O Lord! give Your blessing, we pray, to our work. All our powers of body and mind are Yours and we gladly[85] devote them to Your service. Do then, O Lord, so bless our efforts that they may be a blessing to others; ever promote the Glory of Your holy name and that they may bring forth in us the fruit of true wisdom. Teach us to seek after truth and enable us to gain it: and grant that we may ever speak the truth in love etc.

O Blessed Jesus, who, having fulfilled all that was appointed You of the Father, did finish, in the mystery of Your Passion, the perfect life of Your humiliation upon earth, fill us, we ask You, with a due sense of the dignity and honour of a life of lowly obedience and faithful service; and grant us so to persevere in the work which You have entrusted to us, that, when our earthly course is ended, we may present with the Father the work of a life finished though imperfect, and be accepted for Your merit, who lives and reigns with the Father and the Holy Spirit, God for ever and ever.

Let us offer ourselves wholly to God for His purposes.

133

Almighty[86] and eternal God, from whose presence the angels go forth to do Your will: grant to all Your servants to work for You,[87] who go forth and teach in Your name, and to lead souls to You in obedience to Your commands, that they may serve to Your glory, and that, overshadowed by Your protection and upheld by Your everlasting arms, they, and all they teach, may at last receive the crown of life, through Jesus Christ our Lord, Amen.

O Lord and giver of life, Father of all spirits, as You are all in all, so we would remember all in You, and looking for the time when all shall be brought to You in every deed, we would now bring them to You in prayer. We pray for the whole family of humanity that You would speed the hour when all people shall worship the Son, to the glory of the Father, and live as community,[88] to the praise of the Prince of Peace.[89]

Let us consecrate ourselves afresh to God.

134

Take, Lord, and receive all my liberty, my memory, my understanding and all my will, all I have and I possess. You have given it to me, to You, Lord, I return it: all is Yours. Dispose of it wholly according to Your will. Give me Your love and grace, for this is enough for me.   (St Ignatius)

135
Evacuated children[90]

O Lord Jesus Christ! we ask You by the innocence and obedience of Your holy childhood, by Your reverence and love for little children; guard the children of every land who, in this time of danger, take refuge in the homes of strangers. Keep them from all dangers of body and soul: succour them in temptation; keep them continually in the right way; raise up friends for them; open the hearts of all who receive them, that both protectors and protected may be drawn by Your compelling love more closely to You, who Yourself left Your heavenly home and dwelt as a stranger among humanity.

This we ask for Your own name's sake . . .   (Pleshey, 1940)

136

O Lord Jesus Christ, who took little children in Your arms and blessed them; bless, we ask, all little children dear to us. Take them into the arms of Your everlasting mercy. Keep them from all evil and bring them into the company of those who ever behold the face of Your Father, which is in heaven, and the glory of Your holy name.

137

Lord our God who dwells on high, and yet is well pleased to accept our worship in the earthly house of prayer: look graciously upon all endeavours to renew the outward failures of Your Church and to build new sanctuaries for Your honour and service, and bless all our efforts towards this end in this place. Grant that we may ourselves be built up as living stones in Your heavenly house, and be evermore built together in the mystical body of Your Son, Jesus Christ our Lord, who lives and reigns with You, the Holy Spirit, one God, world without end.

God, who dwells invisible in the heavens and yet for the salvation of humanity manifests Your power on earth, pour down upon this place the light of Your countenance: that all who come hither to seek Your face may truly find You.

138
Weariness

Christ![91] the strength of them that labour and the rest of the weary, grant us when we are tired with our work, to be recreated by Your Spirit; that being renewed for the service of Your kingdom, we may serve You gladly in freshness of body and mind, through Jesus Christ our Lord.[92]

O Holy Spirit, the Comforter, who with the Father and the Son abide as one God, descend this day into our hearts, that while You make intercession for us, we may with full confidence, call upon our Father, through Jesus Christ our Lord.

Let us be anxious for nothing but in everything, by prayer and supplication with thanksgiving, make our requests known to God.[93]

139
Intercessions[94]

Almighty and most merciful Father who has taught us not to think of ourselves only, but also of the wants of others – our king, our country, our rulers, our colonies, we remember before You all Your children in every part of the world who are burdened and oppressed: those whose hopes have been crushed: those whose purposes have been overthrown. We remember all afflicted by poverty or worn down by illness: the sick and suffering, the weary and the heavy laden: those also who are in darkness or despair or who are suffering for righteousness' sake. Help them to rest in You and fully pacify and quieten their souls in You, through Jesus Christ our Lord.

And we commend unto You all those about to depart this life, asking You to grant unto them the spirit of love and tranquillity and trustfulness. May they put their hope in You, and having passed through the valley of the shadow in peace, may they enter into that rest that remains for the people of God, through Jesus Christ our Lord.

We remember also all those once known to us on the earth who have passed into the light of Your presence. Continue Your mercy and loving kindness[95] unto them, we ask You, for evermore. These things we ask through Him who has taught us when we pray to say, Our Father.[96]

140[97]
O God, who are the confidence of all the ends of the earth, grant Your blessing unto all humanity and visit the whole world with

Your mercy. Let Your way be known upon earth and Your saving health among all nations. These things we ask through Him who has taught us when we pray to say, Our Father.

Almighty and everlasting God, by whose spirit the whole body of Your Church is governed and sanctified, receive our supplications and prayers which we offer before You, for all estates of people and especially for Your holy Church, that every member of the same, in their vocation and ministry, may truly and godly serve You, through our Lord and Saviour, Jesus Christ.

O God, the Creator and presence of all humanity, we humbly ask You for all sorts and conditions of people, that You would be pleased to make Your ways known unto them, the saving health unto all nations. There especially, we pray for the good estate of the Catholic Church, that it may be so guided and governed by Your good Spirit, that all who prosper and call themselves Christians may be led into the way of truth and hold the faith in unity of spirit in the bond of peace and in righteousness of life.

Finally we commend to Your Fatherly goodness all those who are in any ways afflicted or distressed, in mind, body or estate: that it may please You to comfort and relieve them, according to their several necessities, giving them patience under their sufferings and a happy issue out of all their afflictions. All this we beg for Jesus Christ's sake.

141

And for these also, O Lord, the humble hearts who bear with us the burden and heat of the day and offer their guiltless lives for the well-being of their country, we supplicate Your great tenderness of heart, for You, O Lord, shall save both humanity and beast, and great is Your loving kindness, O Master, Saviour of the world!

O God, whose presence is everywhere and whose mercy never fails, graciously regard all who are in trouble or danger, and especially: Guide the wanderer, defend the innocent, restore the lost, heal the sick,[98] comfort the bereaved and receive the spirits of the dying.

Lord Jesus, we ask, by the loneliness of Your suffering on the cross, be nigh unto all them that are desolate and in pain or sorrow today: and let Your presence transform their loneliness into comfort, consolation and holy fellowship with You, most merciful Saviour.

O Lord Jesus Christ, who has ordained this holy sacrament to be a pledge of Your love and a continual remembrance of Your Passion: grant that we who partake thereof by faith with thanksgiving, may grow up into You in all things until we come to Your eternal joy.   (R.P.B.[99])

142

God, the Father of our Lord Jesus Christ, of whom the whole family in heaven and earth is named, we Your children who have gathered around Your table remember before You all with whom we have lost in the Communion of Saints and we ask You now to hear our thanksgiving[100] for them.

Look down in mercy upon Your Church militant upon earth, in all its branches and all its ministries. Stir up the heart of all who seek Your kingdom to greater faith and devotion. Draw them nearer to one another in mutual love in the joy of service and guide them back, we pray, to their lost unity, that the seamless robe may no more be torn,[101] nor the body of Christ any more be broken.

You, good Shepherd of the sheep, who in this day have fed us with the precious food of Your sacred body and blood, we praise You, we bless You, we thank You, we adore You. Make us worthy of the channels of Your grace and help us to show forth in our lives that we have been with You, that we live with You, who with the Father and the Holy Spirit live and reign, world without end.

Lord! we remember before You our absent ones. O God![102] author and giver of love, enfold them with us, we ask You, in Your ever-lasting arms for ever and ever. Amen.

To Your loving mercy, O Lord, we commend all whom we love – our relations, our friends, our benefactor, all who are praying for us – all who ask us to pray for them. We pray especially for all those in trouble of any kind – all sick in body or mind, the anxious, the fearful, those who are to spend this night in danger, in pain, in sleeplessness, nurses and doctors watching by the sick.

May Your gracious hand be ever above them, Your everlasting arms below them, and may Your Holy Spirit go with them, lead them onwards to Yourself, through Jesus Christ our Lord.[103]

143

To Your loving mercy, O Lord, we commend all those whom we love – our relations, our kindred, our friends, all who are in sickness or sorrow or distress of any kind, all sinners, all penitents, all for whom we ought to pray and all who pray for us. Bring us all closer together by bringing us all nearer to You.

Lord Jesus Christ, with Your hands we commend all who need and seek our prayers. Be near them to guard them, within them to refresh them, around them to preserve them, before them to guide them, behind them to defend them, above them to bless them.

144

O God! King of Glory, who has exalted Your only Son Jesus Christ with great triumph unto Your kingdom in heaven, we ask You, leave us not comfortless, but send to us Your Holy Spirit to comfort us, and exalt us into the same place to which[104] our Saviour Christ is gone before, who lives and reigns with You and the Holy Spirit, one God, world without end, Amen.

O God! who teaches the hearts of Your faithful people by sending to them the light of Your Holy Spirit: grant us by the same Spirit to have a right judgement in all things and evermore to rejoice in His holy comfort: through the merit of Christ Jesus our Saviour, who lives and reigns with You in the unity of the same Spirit, one God, world without end, Amen.

O God! for as much as without You, we are not able to please You, mercifully grant that Your Holy Spirit may in all things direct and rule our hearts, through Jesus Christ our Lord.

145

Father of all, who has promised to show far more to the prayers that Your children make for one another, let Your loving Spirit strengthen all those for whom we pray. Endue them with the blessing of Your goodness and set a crown of pure purpose on all that they do. Pour into all hearts the spirit of unselfishness, the habit of ungrudging and unwearying kindness in the common cause of this life, that is life indeed. You who are love, let us not be disappointed of our hope, but be it unto us and unto all Your children, according to our faith in Jesus Christ our Lord, Amen.

146

O Lord God almighty! The Creator and Father of all, we yield You hearty thanks that You have ordained for humanity both seed time and harvest and bestow upon us, Your children, the fruits of the earth in their season. For these and all Your mercies, we laud and glorify Your glorious name. Send Your blessing, we ask You, on the farmers and all who work on the land, and succour with Your continual help the present poor plight of the agricultural industry, so vital to the well-being of this nation.[105] Grant such seasonable weather that Your servants may gather in the fruits of the earth and ever rejoice in Your goodness to the praise to Your Holy Name, through Jesus Christ our Lord, Amen.

147

Almighty God, who has promised to hear the petitions of them that ask in Your Son's name, we ask You mercifully to incline Your ears to us, that have made now our prayers and supplications unto You; and grant that these things which we have faithfully asked, according to Your will, may effectually be obtained to the relief of our necessity and to setting forth Your glory, through Jesus Christ our Lord, to whom with You and the Holy Spirit be glory for ever and ever, world without end, Amen.

Almighty God, the foundation of all wisdom, who knows our necessities before we ask and our ignorance in asking, we ask You to have compassion upon our infirmities; and those things which for our unworthiness we dare not and for our blindness we cannot ask, grant them to us, for the worthiness of Your Son, Jesus Christ our Lord.

148

Almighty God, who has given us grace at this time with one accord to make our common supplications unto You, and has promised where two or three are gathered together in Your name, You will grant their request: fulfil now, O Lord, the desires and petitions of Your servants, as may be most expedient for them; granting us in this world knowledge of Your truth, and in the world to come life everlasting, Amen.   (St John Chrysostom)

All that we ask of You,[106] O heavenly Father, we ask in patient confidence and joyful hope, being assured that we ask them according to Your will that[107] the voice of Your Church is heard by You, that the intercessions of the Holy Spirit are known unto You, and that the meditation of Your well-beloved Son, our Lord and Saviour, ever prevails with You.

Therefore we glorify Your name: we fall down before Your throne; we worship and adore Your glorious majesty, evermore praising You and saying: salvation be unto our God, who[108] sits upon the throne and unto the Lamb for ever and ever. Blessing and glory and wisdom and thanksgiving and honour and power and might be unto our God for ever and ever, Amen.[109]

149

Visit us, we ask You, O Lord, with Your loving-kindness and grant that the people of this land, after the example of Your servant St George, may boldly confess the faith of Christ crucified and mercifully fight under his banner against sin, the world and the devil and continue Your faithful soldiers and servants unto their lives' end; through the merits of the same, Your Son, Jesus Christ our Lord, Amen.

150

Almighty God! who has knit together Your elect in one communion and fellowship in the mystical body of Your Son, Christ our Lord, grant us peace so to follow Your blessed saints in all virtuous and godly living, that we may come to Your unspeakable joys which You have prepared for them that unfeignedly love You, through Jesus Christ our Lord.

151

O God! give Your love to the living, Your peace to the dead. Grant unto all the sick and dying Your mercy and Your help from heaven. Receive the souls returning unto You whom You have redeemed with the most precious blood of our Lord Jesus Christ. Let their position be with Your holy apostles, martyrs, saints and lovers in the arms of Christ, in Your peace, in Your eternal kingdom. Grant that their souls may be received by the angels of light and led to the mansions prepared for the blessed. Grant unto them, most merciful Lord, the remission of all their sins, that they may obtain the pardon they have always desired, and make them partakers of the joys of Your heavenly kingdom.

Grant that all Your faithful servants whom You have taken from this earth, may meet You with exceeding joy, and hear the blessed voice of their Master and Saviour in the joyful words: 'Come you, blessed of my Father, inherit the kingdom prepared for you from the foundation of the world.'[110] Grant this, O Father, for Jesus Christ's sake, our only mediator and advocate, Amen.

152

Into Your hands, O Lord, we commend the souls of all the faithful departed, as into the hands of a faithful Creator and most loving Saviour, asking You to grant unto them forgiveness and peace.

Grant to us Lord, in our pilgrimage, the help of their prayers. Grant us the assurance of the Communion of Saints and the joy of their community, that they and we may be for ever one in You.

O Lord, grant us some part and fellowship with Your holy apostles, martyrs, saints and lovers: into whose company, not weighing our merits but pardoning our shortcomings, we ask You to admit us, through Christ our Lord.

153

O Lord, we most humbly ask You, of Your goodness, to comfort all those in trouble or sorrow, or need.[111] Especially we pray for the sick: visit them in Your mercy and heal them, if it be Your will, but above all, grant them the blessed knowledge that in all things, Your will is their peace.

And we also bless Your holy name for all Your servants, who having finished their course in faith do not rest from their labours. And we yield unto You most high praise and hearty thanks for the wonderful grace and virtue declared in all Your saints who have been the choice vessels of Your grace, and the lights of the world in their several generations: most humbly asking You to give us grace so to follow the example of their[112] steadfastness in faith and obedience to Your holy commandments, that at the day of the general resurrection, we and all who are of the mystical body of Your Son, may be set at His right hand, and hear His most joyful voice, 'Come, ye blessed of my Father, inherit the kingdom prepared for you from the foundation of the world.'[113] Grant this, O Father, for Jesus Christ's sake, our only mediator and advocate, Amen.

154

O God, the Creator and Redeemer of all those who believe, may the souls of the faithful departed, through the mercy of God, rest in peace. Rest eternal, grant them, O Lord, and may everlasting light shine on them.

To us also, Your unworthy children, who hope in the multitude of Your mercies, grant some part and fellowship with Your holy apostles, martyrs, saints and lovers, into whose company, not weighing our merits but pardoning our offences, we ask You to admit us, through Christ our Lord.

Let us give thanks for all our lovers of God in the Communion of Saints.[114]

155

O King! Eternal! Immortal! Invisible! who in the righteousness of Your saints has given us an example of godly life, and in their blessedness a glorious pledge of the hope of our calling, we ask that being compassed about with so great a cloud of witnesses, we may run with patience the race that is set before us, and with them receive the crown of glory that does not fade away;[115] through Jesus Christ our Lord.

Almighty God! who has knit together Your elect in one communion and fellowship in the mystical body of Your Son, our Lord Jesus Christ, grant us grace so to follow Your blessed saints in all virtuous and godly living, that we may come to those unspeakable joys which You have prepared for them that unfeignedly love You, through Jesus Christ our Lord, Amen.

O eternal Lord God, who holds all souls in life, shed forth we pray, upon Your whole Church in paradise and upon earth, the bright beams of Your light and heavenly comfort, and grant that we, following the good examples of those who have served here on earth and are at rest, may with them enter into Your unending joy, Who lives and reigns ever one God, world without end, Amen.

156
Thanksgiving for the lives of our elder brothers and sisters, the saints, and for all who have shown us the way

O God, the God of the generations of humanity, we thank You for all who have walked humbly with You, and especially for those near to us and dear, in whose lives we have seen the vision of Your beauty. May we know that in the body or out of the body, they are with You. Make us glad in their living, comfort and teach us through their dying. Unite us still, God of our souls, in one household of faith and love, one family in heaven and upon earth through Jesus Christ our Lord.[116]

Grant us, almighty God, Your peace that passes understanding, that we, amid the sorrows of life, may rest in You, knowing that all things are in You, under Your care, governed by Your will and guarded by Your love, so that with a quiet heart, we may face the clouds and the darkness, ever rejoicing to know that darkness and light are both alike to You, through Jesus Christ our Lord.

Grant us Your love alone with Your grace, and we shall be rich, neither crave for any other blessing.[117]

157
May the love of the Lord Jesus draw us to Himself.
May the power of the Lord Jesus strengthen us in His service.

May the joy of the Lord Jesus fill our souls: and
May the blessing of God almighty, the Father, the Son and the
Holy Spirit be with us and remain with us always.[118]

Go with us in this and all our undertakings and further us with
Your continual help, that in all our doings, begun, continued and
ended in You, we may glorify Your holy name, through[119] Jesus
Christ our Lord.

May God the Father almighty, Father, Son and Holy Spirit, bless
our country, our homes and our friends and ourselves from this
time forth for evermore.

158

Lord! bless us and keep us: the Lord make His face to shine upon
us and be gracious unto us: the Lord lift up the light of His countenance upon us and give us His peace.[120]

Blessed be God: who has not turned away our prayer nor His
mercy from us, Amen.[121]

Blessed be the Lord God who only does wondrous things. And
blessed be His glorious name for ever and let the whole earth be
filled with His glory, Amen and Amen.[122]

The grace of the Lord Jesus Christ and the love of God and the
communion of the Holy Spirit be with us all, Amen.[123]

Grace unto us and peace from God the Father and the Lord Jesus Christ, Amen.[124]

159

And now unto Him who is able to do exceeding abundantly above all that we ask or think, according to the power that works in us: unto Him be glory in the Church by Christ Jesus throughout all ages. World without end, Amen.[125]

Unto Him who loved us and loosed us from our sins by His own blood, to Him be glory and dominion for ever and ever, Amen.[126]

Grace be with us, mercy and peace, from God the Father and from Jesus Christ, the Son of the Father, in truth and love, Amen.[127]

The Lord bless us and keep us: the Lord make His face to shine upon us and be gracious unto us: the Lord lift up His countenance upon us and give us peace. Amen.[128]

Unto Him who is able to keep us from falling and to present us faultless before the presence of His glory with exceeding joy: to the only wise God our Saviour, through Jesus Christ our Lord, be glory and majesty, dominion and power, both now and ever, Amen.[129]

160

The God of peace, who brought again from the dead our Lord Jesus, that great Shepherd of the sheep, through the blood of the everlasting covenant, make us perfect in every good work to do His will, doing in us that which is well pleasing in His sight, through Jesus Christ, to whom be glory for ever and ever, Amen.[130]

The peace of God which passes all understanding keep our hearts and minds in the knowledge and love of God and of His Son Jesus Christ our Lord,[131] and may the blessing of God almighty, the Father, the Son and the Holy Spirit, be with us and remain with us always, Amen.

Grant us Lord, we pray, day by day the joy of true living, that we who seek Your service may find Your peace and grow into the likeness of Your Son, Jesus Christ our Lord.

Appendix: Editing the Prayer Book

In this publication of the *Prayer Book*, I have modernized the language to make it more accessible to readers in the twenty-first century. Changes include: 'Thou' to 'You', 'O Thou' to 'O God' and removing 'Thou' if it is redundant, for example, 'do Thou bless' to 'bless'. Some individual words are modernized. For example, 'fadeth' to 'fade', 'Holy Ghost' to 'Holy Spirit', 'beseech' to 'ask' and 'vouchsafe' to 'grant'. I have also included gender-inclusive language: for example, changing 'men' to 'all' or 'humanity', 'brotherhood' to 'community', plus adding 'and sister' when 'brother' is used. On rare occasions I have changed the word order to make the text flow more easily in contemporary parlance if the meaning is unaffected. In the original *Prayer Books*, Underhill consistently used the spelling 'shewed' for 'showed', echoing Julian of Norwich's spelling. Here I have modernized the spelling to make it more accessible.

Where a small word is accidentally left out (for example, 'a', 'an', 'the'), I have inserted the word. Where Underhill has inserted words above, I have included them in the text. If she provides two or three options for a particular word or phrase, I have provided the latest rendering, as her most mature revision, but I have provided the other option(s) in the endnotes.

Small markings in the text such as a cross or bracket, or a line, written in pencil, have been left out to reduce the endnotes. In addition, I have taken out underlining in the text around authors' names and headings to provide consistency in the text.

In terms of punctuation, I have added commas throughout the text to make the prayers easier to read aloud. I have followed Underhill's lead regarding capital letters in relation to pronouns for God – 'You', 'Your'. In the original *Prayer Books* words such as 'light', when referring to God, were also capitalized. But as this practice is not completely consistent, I have left such words in lower case. We see Underhill's echoes of Teresa of Avila when referring to God as 'Your Majesty', and I have left the capital letters here.

All in all, I have tried to make minimal changes from the original texts but have endeavoured to make the texts more accessible for twenty-first-century readers.

Notes

Introduction

1 Margaret Cropper, *The Life of Evelyn Underhill* (Woodstock: Skylight Paths Publishing, 2003), p. 168.

2 Grace Adolphsen Brame, *The Ways of the Spirit* (New York: Crossroad, 1994), p. 39.

3 Letter from Fr Bill Kirkpatrick to the Warden at Pleshey, 2 June 2004, the House of Retreat archive, Pleshey.

4 I also gained the strong conviction that all royalties go to the House of Retreat at Pleshey, the one Evelyn loved.

5 The earlier *Prayer Book* was not available at my first Pleshey visit. It was donated to Pleshey by Christopher Armstrong, one of Underhill's biographers.

6 On three occasions a prayer is cut in half with a page number in between. In these instances, I have continued the prayer under the first number so that the prayer is easier to access.

7 Charles Williams (ed.), *The Letters of Evelyn Underhill*, 2nd edn (London: Longmans, Green and Co, 1944), p. 196.

8 Christopher J. R. Armstrong, *Evelyn Underhill* (London: Mowbray, 1975), p. 38.

9 Williams (ed.), *The Letters of Evelyn Underhill*, p. 125.

10 Williams (ed.), *The Letters of Evelyn Underhill*, p. 125.

11 Cropper, *The Life of Evelyn Underhill*, p. 30.

12 She wrote in 1931, 'The Lord has put me here, keeps on giving me more and more jobs to do for souls here, and has never given me orders to move.' Williams (ed.), *The Letters of Evelyn Underhill*, p. 195.

13 Lord Ramsey of Canterbury, Foreword to Armstrong, *Evelyn Underhill*, pp. xi–x. Ramsey continues writing that Underhill 'did more than anyone else to sustain the spiritual life in Anglicanism during the interwar period' (p. x).

14 Lucy Menzies, 'Memoir' to Evelyn Underhill, in Evelyn Underhill *Light of Christ* (London: Longmans, Green and Co., 1944), pp. 19–20.

15 Cropper, *The Life of Evelyn Underhill*, p. 102.
16 Von Hügel's three Elements of Religion were a guiding influence in his spiritual direction. Crudely put, the 'Mystical Element' refers to the experiential, the 'Intellectual Element' to the intellectual, and the 'Institutional Element' to the communal, bodily, sacramental element.
17 Cropper, *The Life of Evelyn Underhill*, p. 75.
18 MS VII.143 fo. 196[a–b], St Andrews University Special Collections.
19 Bernard Holland (ed.), *Selected Letters of Baron Friedrich von Hügel 1896–1924* (London: J. M. Dent and Sons, 1926), p. 203.
20 Gwendolen Greene (ed.), *Letters from Baron von Hügel to a Niece* (London: J. M. Dent and Sons, 1927), p. 75. It is not surprising that Underhill recommended *The Imitation* to her own directees (Williams (ed.), *The Letters of Evelyn Underhill*, p. 273).
21 Williams (ed.), *The Letters of Evelyn Underhill*, p. 240.
22 Greene (ed.), *Letters from Baron von Hügel to a Niece*, p. 45.
23 Williams (ed.), *The Letters of Evelyn Underhill*, pp. 163, 220, 271; F. R. Lillie (ed.), *Some Letters of Baron von Hügel* (Chicago: privately printed, 1925), p. 41. Underhill similarly encouraged her own directees to read Grou (Williams (ed.), *The Letters of Evelyn Underhill*, p. 271).
24 Williams (ed.), *The Letters of Evelyn Underhill*, p. 324. Von Hügel describes Fénelon as having helped him 'most directly' with his 'interior life' (Greene (ed.), *Letters from Baron von Hügel to a Niece*, p. 110).
25 Williams (ed.), *The Letters of Evelyn Underhill*, p. 326.
26 Williams (ed.), *The Letters of Evelyn Underhill*, p. 325.
27 Williams (ed.), *The Letters of Evelyn Underhill*, pp. 212, 291.
28 Lawrence Barmann (ed.), *The Letters of Baron Friedrich von Hügel and Professor Kemp Smith* (New York: Fordham University Press, 1981), pp. 242–3. Underhill claimed that Leseur was her model for fitting home life to wider claims (Cropper, *The Life of Evelyn Underhill*, p. 197).
29 *Evelyn Underhill's Prayer Book*, 107, 159.
30 Greene (ed.), *Letters from Baron von Hügel to a Niece*, p. 130. Underhill similarly recommends the psalms to her directees as 'daily food' (Williams (ed.), *The Letters of Evelyn Underhill*, p. 292).
31 Williams (ed.), *The Letters of Evelyn Underhill*, p. 333.

32 Sorella Maria led an ecumenical community of sisters in a Franciscan hermitage at Campello, Umbria, Italy. Underhill visited her in 1925 and corresponded with her intimately.

33 In the original *Prayer Books*, the following prayers are written in Marjorie Vernon's handwriting: 67 (just John Donne poem) and 83.

34 Cropper, *The Life of Evelyn Underhill*, p. 124.

35 Williams (ed.), *The Letters of Evelyn Underhill*, p. 316.

36 Williams (ed.), *The Letters of Evelyn Underhill*, p. 150 (italics added).

37 Menzies, 'Memoir', p. 12.

38 Cropper, *The Life of Evelyn Underhill*, p. 122. The Community of the Servants of Christ built the House of Retreat in 1907 as a convent but outgrew it so it has long been a place of prayer.

39 Underhill was also the first woman asked to lecture in theology at Oxford University in 1921. She received an honorary doctorate in divinity from the University of Aberdeen in 1938.

40 Letter from T. S. Eliot to Audrey Duff, dated 24 July 1941, Faber and Faber files, quoted in Carol Poston's 'Introduction' to *Evelyn Underhill: The Making of a Mystic* (Chicago, IL: University of Illinois Press, 2010), p. xviii.

41 Cropper, *The Life of Evelyn Underhill*, p. 170.

42 Underhill cancelled all retreats in 1935 so that she could focus on writing her book, *Worship*.

43 Examples of her meditations are published in Underhill's *Meditations and Prayers* (London: Longmans, Green and Co., 1949).

44 Menzies, 'Memoir', p. 13.

45 Every spring she sent out a typed slip to her prayerful friends with the dates of her retreats for the year (Menzies, 'Memoir', p. 22).

46 Information about my editing of Underhill's original *Prayer Books* is outlined in the Appendix at the end of this book.

Evelyn Underhill's *Book of Private Prayers*

1 A bookplate here with the title provided is addressed to the Pleshey Warden.

2 The handwriting on the backs of pages is always in a larger, messier font, indicating it was written at a later date.

3 'United' was the earlier word used here. Throughout this *Prayer Book* I am providing the latter word used as Evelyn's more mature work.

4 Initially Evelyn wrote 'Thou art in us'.

5 This prayer is repeated in the later *Prayer Book*. Other repeated prayers are usually stated first in the earlier *Prayer Book* and repeated in the second *Prayer Book*, but at times they are repeated *within* the second *Prayer Book*. Repeated prayers appear on pages 7, 8, 9, 11, 12, 13, 14, 18, 19, 22, 23, 29, 33, 35, 36, 37, 38, 39, 40, 41, 42, 43, 44, 46, 47, 48, 49, 50, 51, 52, 53, 54, 55, 56, 58, 60, 61, 62, 63, 64, 67, 76 and 142. Prayers 14 and 24 are repeated twice.

6 2 Timothy 1.7.

7 The original word 'arrayed' has been modernized.

8 The original word, 'fervour', was used in this line and two lines down. Underhill later changed 'fervour' to 'faithfulness' in both places.

9 John 6.51.

10 The original word was 'nourished'.

11 Ephesians 3.20–21.

12 The original word was 'Majesty'.

13 The original word was 'regard'.

14 The original word was 'refuse'.

15 I have added 'ly' here.

16 Though the word 'them' is not in the original text, I have inserted it as I think it is meant to be there.

17 Translation: 'Restless our heart'.

18 In the original, the phrase 'and given ourselves to things that are vain and false' is written after the word 'grievously'. As it has been crossed out, I have left this phrase out here.

19 The words 'Thus and' are written here then crossed out so I have left the two words out here.

20 Originally it had the word 'all' then 'we' is inserted.

21 The original word was 'prosperity'.

22 The original word was 'adversity' here and in the next line.

23 I have deleted the word 'Sinners' here to help simplify the flow of the language.

24 The original word was 'retreat'.

25 Originally it also had 'for His Service' added here but it is crossed out.

26 Originally it had 'crosses or consolations'.

27 Originally it had 'our' but has 'their' written above. 'Our' is provided as most in keeping with the preceding sentence.

28 The original phrase was 'Smite or heal, subdue or raise us up', but this was crossed out and replaced with 'Give us the bread of life and the bread of sorrow'.

29 The original word was 'perfection'.

30 I have deleted the word 'That' which was originally at the beginning of this sentence.

31 In the original, Evelyn had 'may let charity' but looking at the *Imitation* it is 'wound charity', so it has been changed here.

32 The original word here was 'to'.

33 The word 'charity' was inserted here but is then crossed out in pencil.

34 The original word was 'love'.

35 The original word was 'realization'.

36 Originally Evelyn had 'who art Peace' here.

37 The original words, 'O Christ', were crossed out here.

38 Originally, the word 'Though' preceded 'we', but I've deleted it here.

39 Originally Evelyn wrote 'in Him and through Him we may win the victory over the powers of death and darkness'.

40 The original word was 'healing'. Perhaps this change was made during the Second World War.

41 A final clause 'and ever leaning on Thy arm' has been crossed out so it is not included here.

42 The original phrase was 'not mentioning old offences committed against us nor dwelling upon them in thought, not being influenced by them in heart . . .'. Also, I have deleted the word 'but' before 'loving'.

43 The original word was 'his'. In the next phrase I changed 'him' to 'them' in two cases. I also changed 'neighbour' to 'neighbours' for grammatical reasons.

44 The second *Prayer Book* begins here. In the original, the numbering started again at '1', but here I have changed it so that it continues on from the first *Prayer Book*.

45 Recite the Lord's Prayer.

46 Evelyn originally wrote 'O GOD! Light of the minds . . .' but changed it to what is provided here.

47 The original language, 'fruits meet for repentance', has been modernized.

48 Recite the Lord's Prayer.

49 This heading is written in Old English font in red and black. The first word of each prayer and 'St Francis' is in the same Old English font. The handwriting for the rest of the page is not Evelyn's or Marjorie Vernon's (except for the final paragraph).

50 Luke 24.32.

51 Originally the word here was 'walk' then 'sojourn'. All three options are provided on top of each other with a bracket around them.

52 Evelyn initially wrote 'Galilee' but wrote in the margin 'Judea?'

53 'Ebov' is written here. It is unclear who it is referring to.

54 This is written on a card pasted on to the back page here of the *Prayer Book*.

55 Here Marjorie Vernon writes 'Household' but Evelyn writes underneath it 'Kingdom!'

56 This is most probably Rt Revd Henry Albert Wilson.

57 Evelyn has written 'their' above 'our' with a squiggly line to the left of both words, indicating either word can be used.

58 The numbers 87.1 appear here, presumably a reference to liturgy.

59 Under the word 'Christ' is the word 'God'.

60 In the original, Evelyn had 'true joys' but this was changed by the later 'peace'.

61 Evelyn has written here 'also p. 90', which is page 133 in the revised numbering.

62 Evelyn originally wrote 'sweetly' here with 'brightly' above 'sweetly' with a squiggly line, indicating the reader can choose either word.

63 At this point in the *Prayer Book* we find a piece of paper tucked inside the book, written in a handwriting that is not Evelyn's.

64 The heading for this prayer was originally 'Right Judgment' but it is crossed out.

65 Isaiah 40.31.

66 2 Corinthians 5.17.

67 Psalm 40.3.

68 Psalm 130.6.

69 Here 'Your praises' is in brackets in pencil and in the margin we see the word 'Sanctus'.

70 This handwriting is very neat and could possibly belong to one of Evelyn's friends.

71 This next section is written on a piece of paper found at this place in Marjorie Vernon's handwriting.

72 Book of Common Prayer.

73 Book of Common Prayer (1928).

74 The handwritten word 'Ransom' is very difficult to decipher. The words 'Divine Ransom' are in capitals in the original text.

75 This page and the back of page 72 are written in Italian. I assume they were written by Evelyn's Italian nun friend, Sorella Maria of Campello (1875–1961), who lived at the Franciscan hermitage (*Eremo*) of Campello sul Clitunno, northern Italy.

76 In the original text the words 'be undisturbed' were in brackets here.

77 In the original text the word 'them' was in brackets here.

78 Jude 24.

79 The number 102 is given here.

80 The word 'it' is provided twice in the original text, referring to the words 'our souls' in the prayer in the paragraph above, which is deleted in this published version, as it was a repeated prayer.

81 The words written here then crossed out are 'in this our undertaking' and above that in pencil then crossed out are the words 'Your House'.

82 Originally it had 'from us' but those words have been crossed out.

83 The words deleted here are 'this Retreat'.

84 The words 'in this place' are in brackets.

85 I have changed the archaic expression 'would fain' to 'gladly'.

86 At the top of this page we read in pencil 'see 41'.

87 These four words are written above the line in tiny font and the words 'do any kind of work' are crossed out.

88 I have changed the original word 'brethren' to 'community'.

89 '81' is written in pencil here. 'Soul of Christ 59' is written in a different fountain pen.

90 This prayer was also written on a loose bit of paper found in the *Prayer Book*.

91 Originally Evelyn had the word 'God' but now she's written 'Christ' on top of it.

92 C280 is written as the reference here.

93 Philippians 4.6.

94 Before the heading we read 'also p. 81'.

95 Here 'p. 120' is written.

96 Recite the Lord's Prayer, and also at the end of the next paragraph.

97 'P. 180' is written above the first line below.

98 There is an insert here in the text indicating that you pause to insert the names of any sick people here. This is also the case for those 'bereaved' below.

99 These letters stand for the 'Revised Prayer Book' of the Anglican Church (Book of Common Prayer, 1928).

100 The original word here was 'intercession'.

101 The original word here was the archaic word 'rent'.

102 I have deleted 'who are the' to help the language flow more easily.

103 This prayer was found written on a piece of paper in the *Prayer Book*.

104 The original word was the archaic word 'whither'.

105 A symbol for changing the word order here is used. The original was '. . . industry of this nation, so vital to the well-being'.

106 The original word choice was 'All these things we ask, O Heavenly Father'. Evelyn has a bracket around 'these things' and has indented 'of You'.

107 There is a pencil bracket before 'that' and a pencil bracket before 'and that the meditation . . .'.

108 I corrected the original 'which' to 'who'.

109 Revelation 7.10, 12.

110 Matthew 25.34.

111 The words 'in sickness' have been crossed out.

112 Once again, Evelyn has changed the word order. Originally, the word order was 'follow then the example of . . .'.

113 Matthew 25.34.

114 I have incorporated here a line written above so that the sentence makes sense.

115 The original read 'faded not away'. Hebrews 12.1 KJV.

116 The reference given here is 'Saints 120.115'.

117 The original word here was 'boon'. This sentence is in a different hand-writing, which may be Marjorie Vernon's.

118 Book of Common Prayer.

119 The sentence simply stops here so I have added what is usual in this case, 'Jesus Christ our Lord'.

120 Numbers 6.24–26.
121 Psalm 66.20.
122 Psalm 72.18–19.
123 2 Corinthians 13.14.
124 2 Corinthians 1.2.
125 Ephesians 3.20–21.
126 Revelation 1.5–6.
127 2 John 1.3.
128 Numbers 6.24–26.
129 Jude 24–25.
130 Hebrews 13–20–21.
131 Philippians 4.7.

Index

1   I have combined the indexes of both *Prayer Books* into one and I have made all headings in black even though assorted headings and references were in red font and some were underlined.

Author biographies and liturgical sources

Note: Authors are in order of appearance in *Prayer Books*.

Thomas à Kempis (1380–1471) was the author of the *Imitation of Christ*, written in 1418–27. The *Imitation* is divided into four books providing spiritual instruction and is viewed as the most widely read, devotional book after the Bible.

John Henry Newman (1801–90) was an Anglican convert to Roman Catholicism who became a Catholic cardinal.

H.B. (d. 1577) refers to Henry Bull, the editor of *Christian Praiers and Holy Meditacions*. 'The true pilot' prayer was written by Revd John Bradford (1510–55), an English Reformer and martyr.

Jean Nicolas Grou (1731–1803) was a French Roman Catholic mystical writer.

John Scotus Eriugena (815–877) was an Irish philosopher, theologian and poet.

St Teresa of Avila (1515–82) was a Spanish mystic, Carmelite nun and Roman Catholic saint who wrote several works about prayer.

Edward Bouverie Pusey (1800–82) was an English churchman and a leader of the Oxford Movement.

Pierre de Bérulle (1575–1629) was a French Roman Catholic cardinal and a founder of the French school of spirituality.

Gertrude More (1606–33) was a Benedictine nun who published two works about prayer.

Richard Rolle (1290/1300–1349) was an English mystic, hermit and religious writer who wrote treatises, commentaries and epistles.

St John of Ruysbroeck (1293–1381) was a Flemish mystic, priest and spiritual writer.

Father Baker (1841–1936) was an American Roman Catholic saintly priest.

Bishop Thomas Ken (1637–1711) was an English cleric who wrote *A Manual of Prayers for Young Persons*.

Launcelot Andrewes (1555–1626) was an English bishop and impassioned preacher.

St Anselm (1033–1109) was a Benedictine, Archbishop of Canterbury and scholastic theologian. He is famous for his phrase 'faith seeking understanding'.

St Ignatius of Loyola (1491–1556) was a Spanish priest and theologian. He founded the Order of the Society of Jesus and is known for his *Spiritual Exercises*.

Jean Pierre de Caussade (1675–1751) was a French Jesuit priest and spiritual writer.

Élisabeth Leseur (1866–1914) was a French mystic, best known for her spiritual diary.

St Augustine of Hippo (354–430) was an early theologian, philosopher, bishop and saint.

Nicholas of Cusa (1410–64) was a German theologian, philosopher and mystical writer.

Rabia al-Basri (717–801) was a Sufi mystic and poet.

Ottokár Prohászka (1858–1927) was a Hungarian Roman Catholic religious writer.

Leonine are prayers after Mass that were introduced initially by Pope Leo XIII.

Ambrosian relates to St Ambrose (340?–397), who was a writer and Bishop of Milan.

St Thomas Aquinas (1225–74) was an Italian priest, theologian and Doctor of the Church.

Gregorian relates to Pope Gregory VII (540–604), a Doctor of the Church and a Latin Father.

François Fénelon (1651–1715) was a French Catholic theologian, archbishop and writer.

James Martineau (1805–1900) was an English religious philosopher and writer.

Jeremy Taylor (1613–67) was a Church of England cleric and poetic writer.

St Francis of Assisi (1181/2–1226) was an Italian Catholic preacher and friar who founded the Order of Friars Minor and the Order of St Clare. He was canonized in 1228.

Margaret Cropper (1886–1980) was an English poet, hymnist and author. She was an intimate friend of Evelyn Underhill's from 1931 until her death. Cropper subsequently wrote a biography of Underhill.

Christina Rossetti (1830–94) was an English Victorian poet.

John Donne (1573–1631) was an English cleric in the Church of England and a poet.

Trinity VI refers to the Book of Common Prayer collect for that Sunday.

Alcuin of York (735–804) was an English scholar and poet from York.

Janet Erskine Stuart (1857–1914) was a Roman Catholic nun and educator.

William Law (1686–1761) was a Church of England priest who wrote about practical divinity.

Æthelwold of Winchester (904/9–984) was a bishop and artist and a leader of tenth-century monastic reform in England.

Luis de Leon (1527–91) was a Spanish Augustinian friar, theologian and poet.

Edward Keble Talbot (1877–1949) was an English Anglican priest and the Superior of the Community of the Resurrection, Mirfield. He led some spiritual retreats at Pleshey.

St Basil the Great (329/330–379) was a Greek bishop and theologian and one of the Cappadocian Fathers.

John Eudes (1601–80) was a French priest and missionary. He was founder of the Congregation of Jesus and Mary and the Order of Our Lady of Charity.

Sir Francis Drake (1540–96) was an English sea captain and politician.

St John Chrysostom (349–407) was an early Church Father and Archbishop of Constantinople.

Frances de Chantal (1572–1641) was a Roman Catholic saint who wrote beautiful letters of spiritual direction.

Church liturgies Evelyn Underhill draws upon:

Roman Missal – the liturgical text used for the Roman Catholic Mass.

Leonine Sacramentary – the oldest liturgical text in the Western Latin tradition.

Gelasian Sacramentary – the second oldest Western liturgical book to survive.

Dawn Office, Eastern Church and **Leonine** – liturgy from the Eastern Orthodox Church.

The Mozarabic Rite – a form of worship within the Latin Catholic Church that dates back to the seventh century. 'Mozarabic' relates to the Christians living in Spain under Moorish kings.

Liturgy of Malabar – a liturgy used by Church of Malabar Syrian Catholics.

Monastic Breviary Matins – the ancient monastic Night Office.

The Book of Common Prayer and the **Revised Prayer Book (1928) of the Church of England**.

Veni Creator Spiritus – a hymn written in the ninth century, which is sung in Gregorian chant in Roman Catholic and Anglican churches.

Index[1]